modern tract homes of
Los Angeles

John Eng

Adriene Biondo

4880 Lower Valley Road · Atglen, Pennsylvania 19310

Other Schiffer Books By The Author:
Souther California Eats, 978-0-7643-3332-3, $24.99
Souther California Eats 2, 978-0-7643-3639-3, $24.99

Other Schiffer Books on Related Subjects:
Deco & Streamline Architecture in LA: A Moderne City Survey, 978-0-7643-2008-4, $49.95
Palm Springs Mid-Century Modern, 978-0-7643-3461-0, $29.99
Tour of Frank Gehry & Other L.A. Architecture, 978-0-7643-2715-5, $14.95

Schiffer Books are available at special discounts for bulk purchases for sales promotions or premiums. Special editions, including personalized covers, corporate imprints, and excerpts can be created in large quantities for special needs. For more information contact the publisher:

Published by Schiffer Publishing Ltd.
4880 Lower Valley Road
Atglen, PA 19310
Phone: (610) 593-1777; Fax: (610) 593-2002
E-mail: Info@schifferbooks.com

For the largest selection of fine reference books on this and related subjects, please visit our website at www.schifferbooks.com
We are always looking for people to write books on new and related subjects. If you have an idea for a book, please contact us at the above address.

This book may be purchased from the publisher.
Include $5.00 for shipping.
Please try your bookstore first.
You may write for a free catalog.

In Europe, Schiffer books are distributed by
Bushwood Books
6 Marksbury Ave.
Kew Gardens
Surrey TW9 4JF England
Phone: 44 (0) 20 8392 8585; Fax: 44 (0) 20 8392 9876
E-mail: info@bushwoodbooks.co.uk
Website: www.bushwoodbooks.co.uk

Copyright © 2011 by John Eng and Adriene Biondo

All photos by John Eng unless otherwise noted.

Cover: Burke Residence, Cliff May designer, Lakewood Rancho Estates, Long Beach, 1953

Library of Congress Control Number: 2011929850

Design by John Eng
Type set in Agency FB/Arial
ISBN: 978-0-7643-3865-6

Printed in China

Acknowledgments

We gratefully acknowledge the homeowners who kindly opened the doors of their beautiful homes to us. To those who helped make this book possible, we extend our warmest thanks: Hans Adamson and Amanda Seward, Larry and Frances Beidleman, David and Adeline Block, Robert Burke and Albert Mejia, Alex Carrillo, Chris and Marian Christy, Todd Clark and Carol Bua, Steve and Sandi Clifford, Kevin Daly of Daly Genik Architects, Jeffrey Head, Alan Hess, Merritt Johnson, Bonnie Jones, Elaine Jones, Greg and Anna-Karin Kight, William Krisel, Les Major and Pascale Vaquette, Jeff and Anne Marie Morritt, Charles Phoenix, Doug and Rochelle Kramer, Jon and Kathy Leader, Mark and Gemma Noland, Dianne Phillips, Nick Roberts and Cory Buckner, Steve Rodin, Roger and Casey Russell, Donald Wexler, David Woodruff and Nel Dubrobich,and Dan and Ann Ziliak. Special thanks to our wonderful editor, Jesse Marth.

Disclaimer

Photos, renderings, brochures, or other materials not otherwise credited are from the author's archives/ collection. This book is not sponsored, endorsed, or otherwise affiliated with any of the companies or persons represented herein. This book is derived from the author's independent research.

Contents

Foreword

by Alan Hess

Finally we're getting back to the original vision of Modern architecture: Modern houses affordable to the average buyer.

Sure, Modernism always produced remarkable but expensive custom home designs, like Frank Lloyd Wright's Fallingwater, or Richard Neutra's Kaufmann house. But the heart and soul of Modernism was to place advanced engineering, new materials, and functional design at the service of the average person. You didn't have to be wealthy to enjoy the airy, practical convenience of Modern architecture.

It worked. Developers such as David Bohannon, Fritz Burns, Joe Eichler, Sanford Adler, George and Bob Alexander, and many others brought Modern architecture by excellent architects to tract housing in America in the 1940s, '50s, and '60s. Modern was marketable.

Instead of cracker boxes divided up into tiny rooms, they brought the open plan to Modern suburbanites. Glass walls seamlessly blended the garden with the living areas. Spacious family rooms, re-imagined traditional kitchens, dining rooms, and living rooms as one useful living space. Appliance-bedecked kitchens made cooking a breeze, and the Modern housewife served her children at built-in dining tables with no muss, no fuss.

Mysteriously, though, this fact has been overlooked by historians until recently. The very idea of tract houses and suburban living has been stigmatized so that few observers paid attention to the very tangible advantages of suburban life and Modern houses. The best-known effort by Modern architects to design for the masses (the Case Study Houses of *Arts & Architecture* magazine between 1945 and 1962) went sadly astray; intended as prototypes for average middle class houses, the prices on these prime, pedigreed Modern designs have skyrocketed. The average family could no longer afford the house for the average family—undermining the very purpose of the effort.

Happily, we are rediscovering today (and Adriene Biondo and John Eng's book spotlights) those other long-neglected houses of Modern design out there. Many are still in the midrange of home prices in whatever city they are in. And like the run-down Victorians of fifty years ago, many more are bargains awaiting a good restoration.

Today the stock out there varies for almost any taste and price. There are small legendary tracts like Mar Vista by Gregory Ain on Los Angeles' West Side—but then there is also his little known Park Planned tract in Altadena. There are the well-known tracts of Joe Eichler, but now we have discovered the Modern tracts of the Alexander Company in Palm Springs, designed by Palmer and Krisel and Donald Wexler. Even more recently we've discovered that Palmer and Krisel built many other Modern tracts, such as the Living-Conditioned Homes in the San Fernando Valley by developer Sanford Adler. Architect Edward H. Fickett is finally receiving the attention his Modern tract designs deserve. The prefab Rancho Estates in Long Beach by architects Cliff May and Chris Choate for developer Ross Cortese is now a valued neighborhood—but there are still other May/Choate tracts from Anaheim to Las Vegas to Houston that have yet to be discovered. And the tracts of other architects like Arthur Lawrence Millier and Martin Stern, Jr. are still awaiting suburban archeologists to rediscover them—and home buyers to discover their delights.

Look for simple, Modern wood post and beam or (occasionally) steel structures; the price and ease of Modern assembly-line construction made these houses affordable. So did modularization of windows, doors, bathrooms, and kitchens. Mass produced like cars, toasters, airplanes, or candy bars, these mass produced houses were the ultimate in Modernism. They made good things available to the masses at a reasonable price. So here is the challenge today: there is still no complete list of these tracts. It is up to intrepid Modern home seekers to track them down. They are still there; they have just faded into the background, hidden in plain sight in the suburbs of most cities.

For the tens of thousands of home buyers who yearn for a mid-century Modern home, and who think they must settle for a badly designed Tuscan or a bland Colonial, there is a viable alternative.

Start looking for those open plans, the glass walls and clean eave lines, the balanced natural light from glass clerestory windows, the stylish kitchen appliances of yesteryear, the way the garden flows indoors.

Modernism lived, and it still lives in countless housing tracts.

Introduction

With all the attention that Modern homes have received over the last 15 years or so, do we really need another book on this subject? While it is true that numerous books and magazine articles have been written on the Modern houses of Los Angeles, we found that most tend to focus on custom homes designed by architectural giants such as Frank Lloyd Wright, Richard Neutra, Rudolph Schindler, and architects from the well-documented Case Study Program. Think Modern tract homes and the list of books and articles drops precipitously.

Our aim is not to write the definitive essay on the subject but to hopefully share our enthusiasm via a more subjective, personalized view. Many of the homeowners we feature here are neighbors or friends we have made along the way. While participating in a progressive holiday party one year where party-goers went from one house to the next, covering several different houses in one evening, we were amazed at the variations within the same model—just in our tract alone. It seemed that "standard" models were seldom standard. It soon became apparent that in trying to please demanding home buyers, Joe Eichler often customized the houses in his tracts. And since Eichler was never satisfied with the status quo, he continued to experiment with new designs and materials even while construction was underway. This improvisational approach created unique variations on the models featured in the sales brochures. And while these houses are certainly tract homes, few are absolutely identical to one another. And of course, how individual homes are decorated and furnished can also completely transform them.

We are aware that there are many more Modern tracts in Los Angeles than the five we've included here, but working within the scope of this book, we feel that these five represent a good cross section. While attending home tours and photographing these homes, we felt an immediate kinship to the Modern lifestyle and aesthetic, but just as importantly, we found ourselves wondering who are the people who live in these homes; what do they do for a living and what do they like about them? We discovered that although a large portion of homeowners are in the creative fields; i.e., working as architects, graphic designers, and musicians, there are just as many professionals; i.e., lawyers, psychologists, and school teachers. Among the people we personally know in the Balboa Highlands Eichler tract alone, there are three architects, three graphic designers, a museum curator turned landscape architect, a director of photography, several photographers, an advertising agency creative director, a feature film production designer, two animation directors, a concert violinist, a composer, a fine art painter, a telecine colorist, a grade school teacher, two lawyers, and a coroner. The stories behind the development of these Modern tract homes are fascinating but we find the stories behind these homeowners equally compelling.

Now more than half a century later, not only are these homes of the future still functional and relevant but very much appreciated by a whole new generation of Modern architecture lovers.

Eichler Home, Claude Oakland architect, Balboa Highlands, Granada Hills, 1963.

MODERN ARCHITECTU

THE BIRTH OF MODERN

The Modern Revolution began prior to World War II. In fact, in 1910, before World War I, Frank Lloyd Wright's Prairie house designs were widely seen in the Berlin publication *Ernst Wasmuth*. Designs that integrated cantilevered balconies, wide overhanging eaves, roofs stressing the horizontal (reflecting the flat plains of the American Midwest), and an "organic" sensitivity to their sites heavily influenced the European designers. One in particular was Walter Gropius who would later both design and head the famous Bauhaus school in Germany. This school favored the language of elementary forms, the machine-inspired aesthetic, and the technology of industrial production. Some of the more notable instructors at the Bauhaus were Mies van de Rohe, Marcel Breuer, Laszlo Moholy-Nagy, Paul Klee, and Wassily Kandinsky. With the approaching war and growing disapproval from the Hitler government, Gropius emigrated to the U.S. in 1937 and became the Dean of Harvard's Architecture Department between 1938 and 1952. When Gropius left, Mies van de Rohe took over as Director of the Bauhaus school, but after two years was forced to close the school due to governmental pressures. He then relocated to Chicago and headed the Architectural Department for the Illinois Institute of Technology. Van de Rohe is credited with the most quoted line in Modern design: "Less is more."

Opposite, from top:
Ennis House, Frank Lloyd Wright architect, Hollywood Hills, 1924.

Chrysler Building, William Van Alen architect, New York City, 1928-1930.

Crossroads of the World, Robert V. Derrah architect, Hollywood, 1936.

Another giant of Modern architecture is Le Corbusier. Originally from Switzerland, he traveled all over Europe before settling in France. His revolutionary concepts of "buildings as machines" included ribbon windows, open floor plans, and the influence of the automobile in living and work space, which forever changed architecture.

Two Viennese architects were so inspired by Frank Lloyd Wright's work and non-traditional concepts that they traveled to America in order to work for him. After supervising the construction of two separate textile block houses for Wright in Los Angeles, Rudolph Schindler and Richard Neutra stayed in Los Angeles and opened their own architectural practices. During the 1920s and 1930s, other European architects such as Marcel Breuer from Hungary/Germany, Eliel and Eero Saarinen from Finland, and Albert Frey from Switzerland came to the U.S., where the opportunity to work in the Modern style was welcomed. In the Southwest, the climate in both weather and opportunity proved to be a perfect fit for those who wanted to explore this new style of architecture.

MODERNE

The Paris Decorative Arts Exposition in 1925 inspired the Art Deco movement both in Art and Architecture. This highly decorative style was influenced by the archeological discoveries of the period, from the 1922 discovery of Tutankhamun's tomb in Egypt to Central America's Mayan and Aztec zig-zag lines to the primitive art of Africa. The designs, colors, and motifs were immediately used in this newly revised version and became popularized as Art Deco. The unique style quickly spread throughout the world and you can find Art Deco style buildings in cities from New York to California as well as Oklahoma, Florida, and Cuba. Two of the most iconic examples are New York's Empire State Building and the Chrysler Building. Although the Moderne style is similar to Modern and can be regarded as a cousin, Moderne is more decorative while Modern is simpler, clean-lined, as in "Form follows function."

As early as 1934, homes in the Streamline Moderne style were already being built and sold by developer William P. Kesling in the Silverlake area of Los Angeles.

INTERNATIONAL STYLE

International Style was a term created by Henry Russell Hitchcock and Philip Johnson in 1932 to describe the simple, flat roof, linear designs that transcended nationalities and was thus "International." This style of Modernism was favored by architects Walter Gropius, Mies van de Rohe, Richard Neutra, Raphael Soriano, Craig Ellwood, and Pierre Koenig. From the 1920s to the 1970s, the International style was considered by many to be the quintessential Modern style. The Lever House in New York City, designed by Gordon Bunshaft for Skidmore, Owings, and Merrill, and the Farnsworth House in Illinois, designed by Mies van de Rohe, are classic East Coast and Midwest examples. In Los Angeles, just about anything Richard Neutra designed is likely to be in the International Style.

MODERN DESIGN ELEMENTS

Le Corbusier pioneered the open plan concept in his "Domino" House (1912-1915) project. Starting with a concrete slab, the open floor plan was built on top with a minimal number of thin, reinforced concrete columns around the edges. This design negated the need for permanent weight-bearing walls so that the space remained open to different usages and thus had multiple purposes. If needed, a non permanent "wall" could be used such as a curtain, Venetian blind, accordion screen, or glass door. This concept would later be used by Gregory Ain in the Mar Vista tract. Le Corbusier's theory included five points of architecture:

1. The structure is off the ground using *Pilotis*, or reinforced concrete stilt columns, facilitating efficient storage of the automobile within the structure. These columns also allowed for
2. *Free Facade* or non-supporting, non-permanent walls throughout the building;
3. *Open Floor Plan*;
4. *Ribbon Windows* for unencumbered views of surroundings; and a
5. *Flat Roof* creating additional space for garden, patio, dining, and sleeping areas.

Later his design theories included the use of reinforced concrete, which he then abandoned a few decades later.

Aside from the theories of the enigmatic Le Corbusier (who is considered a genius by some and a crackpot by others), the concepts of Modern design have stood the test of time: Indoor/outdoor living, post and beam construction, concrete slab foundation, skylights, and interior gardens– all of which can be discovered in a Modern tract home. The back of most Eichler homes, for example, is essentially a glass wall where you can experience the outdoors while enjoying all the comforts of being inside.

WORLD WAR II & PRE-FABS

The demand for housing was on even before World War II was over. In California, tens of thousands of shipyard workers and aviation workers created an immediate housing demand that had to be met. The critical need for wartime defense housing led to entire towns springing up almost overnight. With its central location and proximity to wartime aircraft production and industry, the City of Westchester became the site of a major mass housing development created by Fritz B. Burns and business partner Fred W. Marlow. Marlow-Burns took the knowledge they had gained in building mass housing at Westside Village and Toluca Wood and by 1944 had built a Modern, planned community, which could house 10,000 residents. Designers and builders were obsessed with the challenges of how to build better, faster, and cheaper. Both established architects and younger ones wanting to make their mark proposed new ideas and techniques to meet this challenge.

In the early 1940s, mass production was the accepted answer to low cost, affordable housing. After all, wasn't it obvious how Henry Ford's assembly line approach made the ownership of a personal automobile a reality, and how the war was partially won (at least from the home front) by America's ability to out-produce the military machines used during the war? Gregory Ain, who had worked for Richard Neutra in the early 1930s, was awarded a Guggenheim Fellowship to study pre-fabricated housing in 1940. Walter Gropius and Konrad Wachsmann proposed a General Panel System for prefabricated homes that had zero traction on the industry. Eero Saarinen and Olivier Lundquist's proposed Post-War Housing in 1943 using pre-assembled components. Although never built, these WW II defense housing designs were comprised of two sections that when placed together formed a trailer that could be shipped anywhere. Cliff May and Chris Choate offered their "Low-Cost House Building System," a kit of pre-fab parts that could be assembled inexpensively. They sold their designs for $225 to $300 per house. Empirically, it was discovered that while it seemed completely logical that pre-fab homes would cost less, in reality the savings were minimal. Even given the advances in technology and materials over the last 50 years, the total cost of a pre-fab home is almost the same as if the house was built on site. With a pre-fab home, the owner will still have to purchase the property, build a foundation, and install electrical and plumbing prior to transporting the house to the site. According to George Nelson in his book *Problem of Designs*, "a major (and largely hidden) factor was emotional: The house was a sacred cow, a symbol of social status, an outward expression of personality. People already uneasily aware of the gray uniformity gradually enveloping their work, tastes, habits, and thoughts resisted the attack on the house as if industrialization in this area were the final assault on their own disappearing individuality."

Architect Raymond Kappe, who started in 1950 at the office of Ashen + Allen working on Eichlers, is still actively working on solving the affordable mass housing problem. In 2006, he began working with LivingHomes, a developer of healthy and sustainable Modern pre-fab homes. The first LivingHome, designed by Kappe, was the first in the nation to achieve a LEED Platinum rating. Today, there is a resurgence of pre-fab homes with offerings from Marmol/Radziner, LivingHomes, and many others.

From top:
A prefabricated prototype house by architects Marmol/Radziner, Desert Hot Springs, 2005.

A typical Eichler home in Orange County.

Lovell House, Richard Neutra architect, Hollywood, 1929.

EXPERIMENTAL HOUSES

The DYMAXION DWELLING MACHINE was designed by *Buckminster Fuller* in the late 1920s, but was not built until the end of the Second World War. This Swiss army-knife of a house was Bucky's solution to the housing shortage since it would equal the cost of a 1946 Cadillac, or $6,500, be mass-produceable (made to be assemble in a factory like an airplane), and easy to transport (a helicopter could theoretically drop it where you wanted it as it was shipped in its own metal tube). The house was made from aircraft aluminum and was meant to withstand a Kansas tornado. It was round because that shape minimizes material and heat loss while maintaining maximum strength. Features included special O-Volving shelves that operated at the touch of a button. The name "Dymaxion" is the culmination of three words that Fuller used often: dynamic, maximum, and tension. The curved, aluminum structure is reminiscent of an Airstream trailer.

AIRFORM BUBBLE HOUSES were proposed by *Wallace Neff*, a Pasadena architect specializing in the Spanish Medieval style. His resume includes the Gillette Mansion, the Gates Residence, the Libby Ranch, the Pickford Estate, homes for Charlie Chaplin, Cary Grant, and numerous other elites. The Airform Bubble Houses along California Street in East Pasadena were, in 1946, Neff's solution to affordable housing. Also known as a shell, balloon, or concrete dome igloo, Neff began building them in 1941 with what he called "airform construction." A large rubber balloon is inflated, then sprayed with gunite (concrete). Insulation, rebar, and additional layers of concrete are then applied to the shell. Once set, the balloon is removed through the door or windows and reused. In 1941, a dozen of these houses were constructed in Falls Church, Virginia. There were two different designs, single large domes and smaller double domes joined by a hallway. According to Carolyn Fix from a 2007 *Washington Post* interview by John Kelly, "We called the double houses 'bra houses,' because they looked like a bra." Although the houses were built throughout the U.S.A., Mexico, West Africa, Brazil, Pakistan, and the Middle East during the 1940s and 1950s, the demand for Airform houses never actually materialized. Neff himself lived in the only known surviving Bubble House in the United States until his death in 1982. Artist Steve Rodin and his wife bought the Pasadena house in 1998 and are still living there. In the December 1953 issue of *Popular Science*, in a article titled "Life in a Bubble Can Be Beautiful," Harvard trained architect Eliot Noyes described how wonderful it is to live in 600 square feet for only $6,000. Other designs included luxury models with triple bubbles for separate bedrooms, living spaces, and garage. It is noted that "People with hermit complexes, however, shouldn't live in bubble houses."

From top:
Dymaxion House, Buckminster Fuller designer, 1929.

Airform Bubble Houses dubbed "The Bra," Wallace Neff architect, 1941. Photo courtesy of Steve Roden.

Scale is given to the Bubble House by the man in this picture, 1940s. Photo courtesy of Steve Roden.

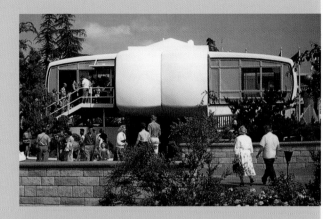

MONSANTO HOUSE OF THE FUTURE. In 1957, the Monsanto Chemical Company sponsored an experimental "Home of the Future" that was almost entirely made of plastic and displayed in Disneyland for 10 years. Designed by MIT architectural faculty members Marvin Goody and Richard Hamilton, this house featured the "Atoms for Living Kitchen" with a brand new type of appliance called the microwave oven. Along with plastic furniture, a dishwasher, intercom system, and closets filled with polyester clothes, the Monsanto House included a giant 21 inch screen television (that did not work).

FUTURO HOUSE. Finnish architect *Matti Suuronen* designed the Futuro House in the mid-1960s completely from fiberglass and plastic. Polykem manufactured these "flying saucer homes" in 1968. Despite selling all over the world (and receiving a positive write-up in *Playboy* magazine), this saucer never really took off. Unlike other pre-fabs, including the Monsanto House, which had plastic cladding over a metal structure, the Futuros were the first structural plastic house. Futuro Houses were delivered completely assembled and brought to the site via a flatbed or helicopter. Using this approach, siting in mountainous terrain with spectacular vistas would no longer be a problem.

Lloyd Turner took the concept of air formed, curved, concrete architecture even further in the 1960s with his "Soap Bubble" architecture. With these torisphere structures, there are flat wall sections as well as curved corners and high ceilings that allow a more efficient use of space.

From top:
Monsanto House, Marvin Goody and Richard Hamilton architects, Disneyland, 1957. Since the wrecking ball just bounced off its surface when it came time for the Monsanto House to leave, it had to be disassembled piece by piece. A pity and a loss for all of us. Photo courtesy of Charles Phoenix.

Futuro House, Matti Suuronen architect, Pine Cove. This particular house was not delivered to the mountainous site via helicopter but by conventional flatbed truck up a curvaceous San Jacinto mountain road.

POST WORLD WAR II HOUSING

America emerged victorious and with a new sense of optimism. It was time to rebuild the country. Returning GIs were eager to pick up where they left off just before the war, anxious to start their own families and launch new careers. The federal government knew it had an important role to play in rebuilding the country. In response, they offered generous home loans to war veterans and tax benefits for homeowners. At the same time, President Eisenhower advocated a progressive highway system and promoted the automobile. He knew that new industries would be created in response to the demand for new homes. These industries would create jobs for Americans who would in return buy the very products that they were making: houses, appliances, furniture, and automobiles. Other interconnected industries would also be created or given a shot of adrenalin as advertising, communication, entertainment, manufacturing, along with the recreation and tourist trade, blossomed throughout the country.

During World War II, materials were heavily rationed and steered toward the war effort, but after the war, not only were these materials available, but newly developed materials such as plastics were now ready to be exploited by private companies for an eagerly awaiting domestic consumer market. Factories were converted as technologies and materials used for the war were then applied to the civilian sector. Industries from home construction, metal, lumber, chemical, oil, transportation, appliances, furniture, and communication to entertainment focused on the everyday consumer. New materials such as fiberglass, laminated plywood, plastics, Formica, masonite, and vinyl and asbestos floor tiles, along with tried-and-true materials like steel, aluminum, rubber, glass, wood, and brick were now made available to everyone. Steel beams and trusses, aluminum extrusions, metal decking, concrete, and fluorescent lighting usually applied in factories were now put to home use. Progressive architects like Charles Eames, Pierre Koenig, and Donald Wexler took advantage of the availability of these postwar materials and began designing homes around them.

Case Study #21, Bailey House, Pierre
Koenig architect, Bel Air, 1959. One of the
most celebrated and published Modern
houses in all of Los Angeles. A study in
simplicity and elegance. A gorgeous
reflecting pool almost completely surrounds
this steel frame masterpiece.

Opposite:
Case Study #16, Craig Ellwood designer,
Bel Air. A classic Miesian glass box with
steel frame structure. Here, Ellwood uses the
frosted glass screen to maintain both privacy
and his Modern design principles.

CASE STUDY HOUSE PROGRAM

In 1940, John Entenza took over as editor of *Arts & Architecture* magazine. He retooled the

magazine to champion and promote the Modern aesthetic. His all-star advisory board members

included Walter Gropius, Marcel Breuer, Victor Gruen, Richard Neutra, Welton Becket, Whitney

Smith, A. Quincy Jones, Raphael Soriano, Gregory Ain, George Nelson, Garrett Eckbo, Esther

McCoy, Pierre Koenig, and Craig Ellwood. Entenza also had the very talented designer Alvin

Lustig on staff. In five years, *Arts & Architecture* served as a launching platform for the famous

Case Study House Program. Within the context of this program, Entenza would showcase and

promote the works of young innovative architects. Many, like Charles and Ray Eames, would

also serve as their own client/guinea pig, as well as architect.

This classic art-directed ad from the May 1957 issue of *House & Home* is using this stylish couple to sell their fantastic new material, Formica.

Opposite, from top:
Not only did Celotex supply building materials such as lumber, roofing shingles, insulation sheathing, and wallboard, but they also offered home designs in their brochures. Styles ranged from Western Ranch to Tri-level design to flat-roof Contemporary (Modern) plans.

A typical fiberglass ad from the 1940s.

TRACT HOME BUILDERS

Hundreds of Merchant Builders (the term for tract home builders of the period) spread across America during the postwar period. They were building tens of thousands of houses at the same time. On the East Coast, one of the most prolific developer/builders was Levitt & Sons. Their best known tract included 17,000 homes in their famous Levittown, between New Jersey and Pennsylvania. These developments were not just houses, but entire communities that included schools, hospitals, churches, recreation areas, and shopping centers. In a 1950s ad for General Electric appliances, these houses were advertised for $17,500 with $100 a month covering all taxes, interest, and insurance, with only $1,000 down for veterans and $2,600 for non-veterans. Included at no extra cost was a brand new nine and a half foot *Wonder Kitchen* by General Electric.

In postwar California, developer Fritz B. Burns partnered with industrialist Henry J. Kaiser to establish Kaiser Community Homes. They advertised "22 Miles of Homes" to be built in the heart of the vast San Fernando Valley. The "City Within a City" garnered national recognition, winning the annual National Association of Home Builders' "Best Neighborhood Development" competition in 1949. In the 1950s, builders Louis Boyer and Mark Taper bought 3,375 acres in Lakewood and built Lakewood Park, a community for 70,000 people and 17,000 homes, even more extensive than Levittown. While most of these tract homes were built in the popular Traditional and Ranch Styles, there was a Modern storm emerging on the horizon.

Throughout the 1950s, Modern tract homes were made available by many builders across the United States. A short list would include David Bohannon (Northern California), Henry Doelger (Westlake, Northern California), George and Robert Alexander (Southern California), Joseph Eichler (Northern and Southern California), John F. Long (Phoenix, Arizona), Edward Hawkins (Denver, Colorado), Howard Grubb (Oklahoma), Don Scholz (Toledo, Ohio) and Robert Davenport (Alexandria, Virginia).

In Southern California, Eichler Homes built a total of five tracts, one in Los Angeles County, three in Orange County, and one in Ventura County. Paul Trousdale of Trousdale Estates built over 25,000 homes throughout the Southland in Beverly Hills, Palm Springs, Long Beach, Wilmington, Compton, and the San Fernando Valley, many with Modern architect Edward Fickett. Westmont Estates, located in the Pomona Valley just east of Los Angeles, boasted as being the first "Modern" tract in the United States to be financed by the Federal Hosing Administration (FHA). They were constructed in 1950 with designs by Arthur Lawrence Millier. "Histotainer" (historian-entertainer) Charles Phoenix wrote in his book *Cruising the Pomona Valley*, "The uncluttered look featured floor to ceiling picture windows, Formica counters, Waste King garbage disposals, and contemporary colors…the model homes decorated by Barbara W. Millier were stylishly furnished with Eames and Paul McCobb." Priced just below $10,000, these houses included three bedrooms and were featured on the cover of *The Los Angeles Times Magazine*.

These Modern ranch designs are just a couple of examples of the many styles offered by Celotex.

For over 40 years, the Alexander Construction Company the father and son team of George and Robert Alexander, built tract homes in both Los Angeles and Palm Springs. In the San Fernando Valley, the Alexanders hired architects Dan Palmer and William Krisel to design numerous tracts of Modern homes throughout the 1950s. The Alexanders also hired Palmer and Krisel to design houses in Palm Springs. In addition, they worked with Wexler & Harrison to build a unique community of steel houses in the northern part of Palm Springs. Sadly, George and Robert Alexander died in a plane crash on November 14, 1965, but the Alexander's legacy is secure, particularly in Mid-Century Modern Palm Springs.

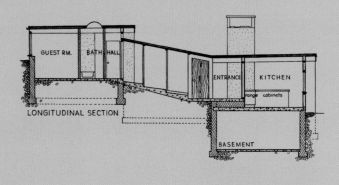

LONGITUDINAL SECTION

BASEMENT

GUEST RM.   BATH HALL   ENTRANCE   KITCHEN
range   cabinets

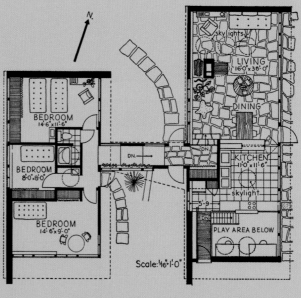

N.

skylights

LIVING
16'-0" x 38'-0"

DINING

BEDROOM
14'-6" x 11'-6"

BEDROOM
8'-0" x 8'-0"

DN.

KITCHEN
11'-0" x 11'-6"

skylight

BEDROOM
14'-6" x 9'-0"

5'-9"

PLAY AREA BELOW

Scale: 1/16"=1'-0"

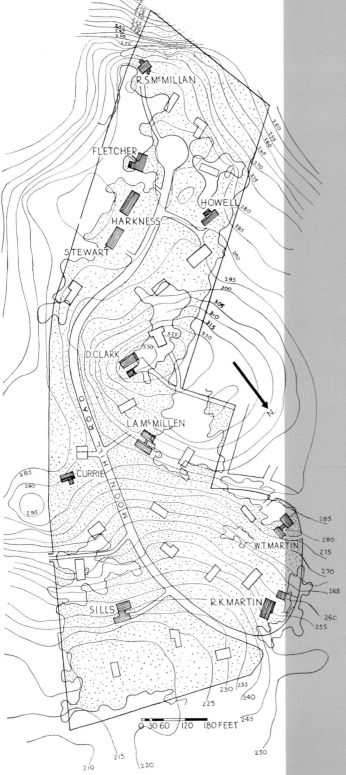

Site plan for the Six Moon Hill
Collaborative, two miles from
Lexington, Massachusetts.
TAC The Architects
Collaborative, 1948.

24

COOPERATIVES

Another form of home development is a cooperative, or co-op. Here, a group of people with similar interests come together to plan and build their home and community. Cooperatives originated as an attractive idea since residents would not only be able to guide the design of their new homes but would also be involved in the design of the very community they would be raising their families. These residential communities also included schools, recreation centers, shopping centers, post offices, churches, etc. Investors would save money by buying larger lots of land and larger quantities of materials at one time. Design costs would be shared and after World War II, the FHA often assisted with financing. Modern cooperatives popped up all over the United States. In Colorado, there was the ADC Skyway Development in Colorado Springs and the Mile High Cooperative in Denver. In Pleasantville, New York, The Usonia was headed by its principal designer and coordinator David Henken, who was a student of Frank Lloyd Wright. Also in New York, the 21 Acres Cooperative in Ardsley included a doctor, architects, an architectural photographer, and industrial designers. In Los Angeles, the Mutual Housing Associates, Inc. was created by several musician friends who hired architects A. Quincy Jones, Whitney R. Smith, and Garrett Eckbo. One of the most environmentally and socially conscious housing tracts proposed after the war was the Community Homes cooperative with planner Simon Eisner, architect Gregory Ain, and landscape architect Garrett Eckbo. The proposal was for 280 units on one hundred acres in Reseda, California. Three years went into its planning before it was killed by Regulation X, which prevented the FHA from financing the project due to their open race policy. At the time, it was generally believed that mixed races would bring down property values. Although the development never broke ground, many of the design ideas were applied directly to the Mar Vista Tract in 1948.

Similar to a cooperative is the collaborative. With Five Fields in Lexington, Massachusetts, the designers were also the builders. Here, The Architect's Collaborative, or TAC, consisted of architect Walter Gropius and a group of young men and women working collaboratively to design and build a community they wanted to live in. In the late 1940s, TAC bought a 20-acre site and built 11 Modern homes in Six Moon Hill, two miles from Lexington, Massachusetts.

HOW CALIFORNIA INFLUENCED MODERN DESIGNS

THE CLIMATE

Since Southern California boasts of more than 300 sunny days a year with an average temperature in the mid 70s, the concept of indoor/outdoor living was only natural. In 1920, Frank Lloyd Wright hired Rudolph Schindler to supervise the construction of the Hollyhock House for Aline Barnsdall in Los Angeles. A year later, Schindler decided to build a house for himself where he could experiment with new ideas. The group of free spirited artists and socialites that he was a part of included Dr. Philip Lovell, a Naturopath and a key promoter of health through outdoor living. After a camping trip in Yosemite National Park, Schindler was so inspired by the beauty and climate of California that when he built his own home in West Los Angeles on Kings Road, he considered the entire lot as his living space. The concrete slab was on the same level as the surrounding grounds. Sliding screen doors could be removed during warm weather so as to maximize the flow between the exterior and interior. Initially, Rudolph and his wife, Pauline, shared the house with another couple, the Chases, who were artists from Chicago. While the two couples did have separate bedrooms, the sleeping quarters were on the roof of the house, with no walls, more along the lines of a carport than a typical enclosed bedroom. This was indoor/outdoor living at its best. Later, Eichler's use of the atrium allowed a similar feeling of being inside and outside while maintaining privacy. During the Case Study House period, Craig Ellwood used frosted glass screens as the answer to the privacy problem while maintaining his Miesian glass box concept. With the frosted screen set several feet away from the house, the person inside the house can still look out his glass wall and prance around completely naked if he or she wishes! And since it almost never snows in Los Angeles, the flat roof of the International Style was a perfect fit, much more suitable in Southern California than in Eastern cities like Chicago or New York. A flat roof can serve multiple purposes by creating an outside patio with reflecting pools (as in many of Neutra's designs) and enclosing the rest of the house.

This typical Southern California winter sunset exemplifies the indoor/outdoor living concept. The Desert House, a prefab home in Desert Hot Springs. Marmol Radziner architect, 2005.

Opposite:
Chemosphere House, John Lautner architect, 1960. The 180-degree view of the San Fernando Valley from this house is spectacular on a clear day.

"Eons ago Mother Nature blessed Southern California with a more than generous serving of her finest fair weather, fertile valleys, sunny shores and snow-capped mountain peaks."

–Charles Phoenix from *Southern California in the 50s.*

LAND & TERRAIN

Aside from a near perfect climate, there was an abundance of land in California in the early twentieth century. Architectural photographer Julius Shulman recalled how when he was a young boy living in Los Angeles during the 1920s, his family would take weekend trips to the beach. There, they would run into real estate salesmen who offered free lunches in exchange for the opportunity to show the Shulman family properties that were available at the time.

Another influence is the topography of Los Angeles. The city is so diverse that an ad in 1897 showed a group eating oranges at an orchard at 10:15 A.M., then engaging in a snowball fight (presumably up in Mount Baldy) at 11:30 A.M., and the same group frolicking in fashionable 1920s swimwear at a Santa Monica beach at 3:30 P.M.! Los Angeles has flat land, hills, valleys, snow-capped mountains, and miles of coastline, not to mention spectacular ocean views. A hillside lot with a 45 degree slope offered architect John Lautner a challenge in 1960 which he could not resist. Lautner's answer was the iconic Chemosphere House, an octagonal house resting on a single concrete pylon secured to bedrock. Some have described this house as a flying saucer about to take off and it's easy to see why, just watch a classic 1950s sci-fi film like *Earth Versus the Flying Saucers.* In a *Los Angeles Times* survey from 2008, the Chemosphere House was listed as one of L.A.'s Top 10 houses.

CALIFORNIA LIVING

California was the land of plenty. Starting with the Gold Rush of 1849, the state quickly became an agricultural mecca during the late 1800s with crops of citrus, walnuts, grapes, and olives. Oil was discovered in 1892 and the second population boom was underway. In 1913, William Mulholland brought water from the Eastern Sierra and the Colorado River via aqueducts, an engineering feat that was rated second only to the Panama Canal. The Pacific Electric or Red Line served the people of Los Angeles, the Sante Fe Railroad connected California to the East, the Southern Pacific Railroad connected California to the North, and the Port of Los Angeles and the Port of Long Beach connected Los Angeles to the world. Early in the twentieth century, filmmakers headed west to California to capitalize on the great climate, diverse terrain, and in order to avoid technical patents and East Coast shakedown. By the end of World War I, Los Angeles had become the movie capital of the world. Around the same time, a modest aircraft industry began with Donald Douglas and the Lockheed brothers, exploding into a major industry during World War II when Southern California produced more aircraft than any other state in the country. Los Angeles became home to McDonnell Douglas, Hughes Aircraft, Lockheed Aircraft, Northrop, North American Rockwell, Rocketdyne, Jet Propulsion Laboratory, and California Institute of Technology. During the post World War II years, President Eisenhower promoted the automobile and a progressive highway system, knowing its role was essential to the rebuilding of the country. Directly and indirectly the promotion of the automobile created jobs for millions of Americans. Thousands of Americans worked in car manufacturing plants while roads and highways were being constructed. The workers who bought the very cars they helped build drove them across America on vacations, which in turn fed the tourism industry. Natural resources like Yellowstone and Yosemite National Park were marketed across the country and Americans ate it up like apple pie. And what would a vacation be if you couldn't share all those wonders with family and friends? Now, not only could you tell others but with a little help from Kodak, Bell & Howell, Argus, Keystone, and Revere, you could *show them* in living color via Kodachrome slides or 8mm home movies. Forcing photo albums, slide shows, and

NORTH AMERICAN AVIATION. INC.

City of Gracious Living
(Continued From Page Nine)

Its advantages for better living likewise make Downey an unusually favorable site for industry. Industry has already discovered this. Three large

plants, each with a payroll in the high thousands, add much to the area's economy. A number of small and medium sized manufacturing plants bring further variety and stability.

There is room and there are all the essential resources for many more.

Left: The Navajo missile, produced at Downey, now being used for "Research in Supersonic Environments" program.

Right: Downey's prize-winning float, Tournament of Roses, 1958.

Below Rio Hondo Golf Course.

PHOTO BY HAL LINK

A page from the booklet published by the Downey City of Commerce, circa 1950s. Back then, life was nothing but fun, golf, and rockets. Original brochure courtesy Analisa Ridenour.

This classic "Dingbat" apartment illustrates the utility of the carport, the decorative theme (in this case it's located on Hauser Street), and the quintessential dingbat lighting fixture.

home movies upon friends and relatives during parties and barbecues became a regular ritual. The advertising industry during this period experienced a major boom thanks to an endless line of new products that were now available. The Cold War and Space Race after World War II created an aerospace industry that provided jobs to tens of thousands of Americans, many in Southern California.

With the construction of the freeway system in Southern California, the automobile became the centerpiece of this new American Dream. In postwar Los Angeles, another population boom poured over the earlier boom. Urban planner John Chase pointed out that Los Angeles' population increased by two million during each decade of the 1940s and 1950s and apartment construction reflected this trend, "...greater than ever numbers of them were built in the period from 1952 to 1966, peaking in 1962-63 at 2,300 permits per year."

Not everyone could afford to buy their own home. In order to mitigate the housing demand, thousands of inexpensive apartments popped up over the Southland throughout the 1950s and 1960s. These simple structures have affectionately become known as *Stucco Boxes* or *Dingbats*. Usually nothing more than simple wood structures covered in stucco, Dingbats are typically two to three stories high with themed fronts, lush

gardens and a swimming pool in the center courtyard. Many include large Modern light fixtures on the front façade (thus the name Dingbat) and an overly romantic/fantasy name like Aloha Gardens, Flamingo Capri, Tradewinds, Kona Pali, Caribbean, The Golden Mermaid, Riviera Villa, Taj Mahal, Stardust, El Matador, The Cinema, or The Starlet. Despite the endless variety of themes and styles such as Polynesian, Modern, Ranch, Colonial, Spanish, etc., they share one common element that is rooted in the efficient use of space (or how to stretch your dollar, depending upon how you look at it). The use of the carport or semi-underground parking is another classic way to maximize the square footage. It is interesting to note how this is one of the five points contained in Le Corbusier's theory on Modern design. One of the most prolific architects of this type of ubiquitous dwelling was Jack Chernoff, with more than 2,000 buildings to his credit.

Culturally, the Golden State attracted people who wanted to work hard, take risks, and were proud to be different (even amongst others that felt the same way). Even East Coast Beatniks were attracted to the West Coast, where freedom of expression was not only encouraged but considered an innate right. By mid-century, the California myth as personified in the Mamas and Papas song *California Dreaming* was solidly affixed, not only in the United States but throughout the world.

With perfect weather, palm trees, Modern folded-roof dwellings by Donald Wexler, and a crystal clear swimming pool to sun bathe and sip your tropical drinks by, life can get no better. Palm Springs, 1950s.

Opposite:
The hyperbolic paraboloid offered a counterpoint to the International Style of Modernism. This organic style relates to Oscar Niemeyer's curvy, free-formed aesthetic as well as the flamboyant shapes of the commercial Googie style.

ARCHITECTURAL STARS OF SO CAL MODERN

Many giants of Modern architecture worked in Southern California. Starting with Frank Lloyd Wright, whom William Krisel called "the god of modern architecture," to Irving Gill, Lloyd Wright, R. M. Schindler, Richard Neutra, and John Lautner to the influential University of Southern California School of Architecture, where Modern architects such as Whitney R. Smith, Louis Armet, Eldon Davis, Conrad Buff, III, Donald C. Hensman, Edward A. Killingsworth, Pierre Koenig, William Cody, William Krisel, Richard Dorman and many more got their education. Others like Gregory Ain, Raphael Soriano, Rodney Walker, William S. Beckett, Carl L. Maston, Raymond Kappe, Raul Garduno, and so many more contributed immensely to the Modern landscape of Southern California. Although some were affiliated with the renowned Case Study House Program, many were not. In nearby Palm Springs, local talent included John Porter Clark, Albert Frey, E. Stewart Williams and Donald Wexler.

Although numerous architects worked in both residential and commercial, some worked exclusively in commercial. Their contributions to Modern architecture, however, should not be overlooked. Douglas Honnold, Welton Becket, Paul R. Williams, Victor Gruen, William Pereira, Charles Luckman, A. C. Martin, and Edward Durell Stone are just a few, not to mention Moderne designers like Milton Black, Stiles O. Clements, and S. Charles Lee, who has been credited with designing more than 400 movie theaters from the 1920s to the 1940s.

Another Modern heavyweight is Cliff May. Although not a licensed architect, he worked with architect Chris Choate to design more than 18,000 tract homes and 1,000 custom homes. And two rather underrated architects are Martin Stern, Jr. and Ralph A. Vaughn. In addition to designing the Ship's and Jack's restaurants in Los Angeles, Stern designed the Encino Village tract on the former RKO Studios lot. Ralph Vaughn, an African-American architect, worked with famed Modernist landscape architect Garrett Eckbo on Lincoln Place, a garden style apartment complex in Venice, California.

EICHLER HOMES
BALBOA HIGHLA

IN
NDS

granada hills

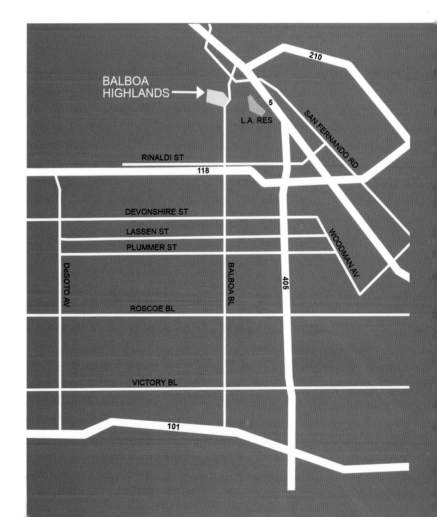

BALBOA
HIGHLANDS

210

5

L.A. RES

SAN FERNANDO RD

RINALDI ST

118

DEVONSHIRE ST

LASSEN ST

PLUMMER ST

DeSOTO AV

BALBOA BL

405

WOODMAN AV

ROSCOE BL

VICTORY BL

101

EICHLER HOMES HEADQUARTERS • 2151 ST. FRANCIS DRIVE • PALO ALTO • DAVENPORT 1-

EICHLER HOMES IN BALBOA HIGHLANDS
Tract: BALBOA HIGHLANDS
Builder: EICHLER HOMES
Architects: A. QUINCY JONES, FREDERICK EMMONS, & CLAUDE OAKLAND
Location: GRANADA HILLS, CA
Year: 1962-1964

EICHLER HOMES IN BALBOA HIGHLANDS

In the early 1940s, Joseph Eichler was a successful executive at Nye and Nisson, Inc., the most successful independent butter and egg wholesaler in the Bay Area. But two overlapping events changed his life. The first dates back to 1943, when Eichler rented the Bazett House, which was designed by Frank Lloyd Wright. The second event occurred in 1945, when the president of Nye and Nisson and three employees were charged and convicted of defrauding the federal government. Eichler was not involved but the trial allowed him the opportunity to reflect upon his life. While living in the Bazett House, he realized how unhappy he had been during his last 20 years as Chief Financial Officer. So at age 45, he launched into his second career as a builder of economical homes, applying what he had learned and enjoyed from living in a Modern house.

After hiring Ashen and Allen to design Eichler's own home, Eichler hired the same architects to design his very first tract homes in Sunnyvale and Palo Alto, California. Although these tracts sold well, a dispute between the architects and Joe Eichler over compensation resulted. In the December 1950 issue of *Architectural Forum*, one of the Eichler tracts was cited as the Subdivision of the Year. In the same issue, A. Quincy Jones won first honor in residential architecture from the American Institute of Architects for a prototype house he designed for A. C. Hvistendahl. It seemed that Jones and Emmons were destined to work together. As part of the original design team while at Anshen and Allen, Claude Oakland had been working on the Eichler tracts from the very beginning. Unlike his employers, Oakland was able to satisfy the economical demands of merchant building (tract building) while not sacrificing any artistic Modern principles. In the early 1960s, Claude Oakland formed his own architectural studio and worked for Joe Eichler directly.

In Southern California, Eichler announced the grand opening of the Fairhaven tract in the City of Orange on February 5, 1960. In May 1962, Eichler broke ground on the Balboa Highlands tract in Granada Hills. The Conejo tract (the last Eichler tract in Southern California) in Thousand Oaks followed in 1964. Of the five Southern California tracts (three in Orange County, one in Ventura, and one in Los Angeles), the Balboa Highlands tract is the only Eichler tract built in Los Angeles County. The residents of Balboa Highlands are now proudly living in a historic neighborhood, officially listed in 2010. Balboa Highlands is the 25th Historic Preservation Overlay Zone in Los Angeles and the very first postwar neighborhood in the San Fernando Valley to attain historic status.

DESIGNS

Balboa Highlands is a beautiful tract of just over 100 homes built on a knoll that was once an orange grove. Underground utilities mean there are no unsightly telephone poles throughout the neighborhood. Balboa Highlands features three basic floor plans: a classic post and beam with a flat roof, a low gabled design, and a third model with a center gable, as well as several prototypes. A spacious open plan, post and beam construction with curtain glass walls and the atrium are just a few of the Modern design concepts you find in an Eichler home. Heat, plumbing, and electrical systems are all contained within the slab foundation. Materials such as Douglas fir beams, redwood ceilings, Philippine Mahogany paneling, decorative block or brick for fireplaces, grooved wood siding, sliding glass doors, Sky Dome skylights, and expansive glass walls are standard issue here. The atrium, which was introduced in the late 1950s, remains one of the most unique features of an Eichler. This enigmatic element can be found in classic Greek structures and throughout Asia and is a truly private indoor/outdoor living space that can be personalized to individual tastes.

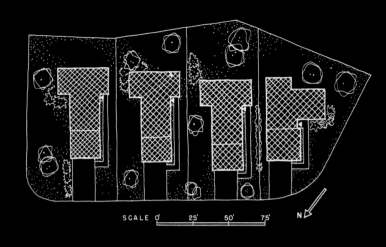

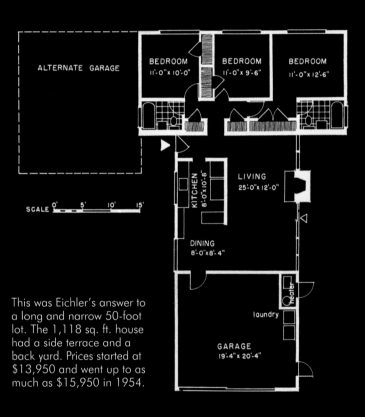

This was Eichler's answer to a long and narrow 50-foot lot. The 1,118 sq. ft. house had a side terrace and a back yard. Prices started at $13,950 and went up to as much as $15,950 in 1954.

In a January 1954 *House & Home* article, Joseph Eichler was selling his backyard as an "outdoor living room." Looking out from the living room at the Thomas Church/Katherine Stedman landscape that came with their house, one can easily believe this. While the front of Eichler homes tends to be extremely low profile with little to no windows, the rear of the house is typically floor-to-ceiling glass.

Beidleman Residence

Larry Beidleman worked as an engineer/designer in Advance Design and System Integrations for the Douglas Aircraft Company in Santa Monica before he retired in 1982. In the 1940s, he worked in the Aviation and Missile and Space Systems Division. One of his last major projects was Skylab. Since his early teens, Larry has been split between his love for architecture and aviation, so even after he began working for Douglas, he decided to commission Case Study architect Pierre Koenig to design a two story steel house for him and his wife Frances. Larry had purchased a plot of land in Kenter Canyon, the same location as the Mutual Housing project. The Beidlemans went so far as to have a scale model built, though the stability of the hillside turned out to be questionable. And while the cost of $60,000 was do-able, it was a bit high. At the same time, Frances and her mother were driving the brand new San Diego (405) Freeway, when Frances noticed signs directing them to the newly completed Eichler tract. Frances was very excited about what she saw and when she returned home, she told Larry all about these Modern houses that were bigger while only *half* the price of the one proposed by Koenig. The instant Larry visited the tract, he agreed that they had found their future home. The Beidlemans purchased their Eichler in 1963 for $38,000. When they moved in, they invested in Knoll and Eames furniture which they still use today, along with the original electric stove that came with the house. Larry custom built a sheet metal exhaust vent over the stove and a custom mailbox that mirrors the central gabled "A" of their classic Jones & Emmons designed Model AQJ-1505.

Plan 1505

FOUR BEDROOMS, 2 BATHS, PARLOUR AND DINING ROOM, KITCHEN, MULTI-PURPOSE ROOM, RETREAT, ATRIUM, GARAGE AND CARPORT.
SQUARE FOOTAGE: LIVING AREA 2515, GARAGE 285, CARPORT 315

Note how Larry Beidleman's homemade mailbox reflects the shape of his Jones & Emmons Eichler.

Frances and Larry admiring the camellias in their atrium.

Over tea, the couple told us how they came to find their ideal home in 1964.

Larry at Douglas during the "good old days."

41

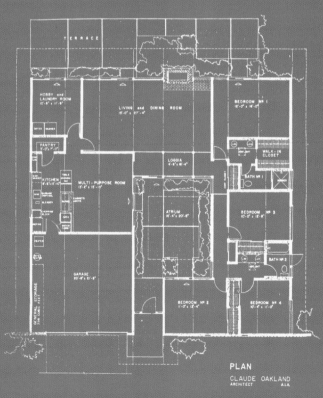

PLAN

CLAUDE OAKLAND
ARCHITECT   A.I.A.

Block Residence

David Block has said he has nine lives. In a previous career he was a real estate agent and had seen many houses of all types, but when he saw this Eichler on Nanette Street in foreclosure in 1993, it was "Eureka!" Fortunately, his wife Adeline, shares his enthusiasm for Mid-Century Modern. Adeline is studying for the bar and David is a colorist for a post production company restoring and transferring old movies into digital format. Their Claude Oakland Model LA-374 offers an open feeling rarely found in a traditional home. The couple spent years methodically restoring their Eichler while trying new materials and different ideas. In keeping with the spirit of the Modern design, they maintain the original ball light fixtures and general footprint of the house while decorating the interior with Modern furniture and art. In their family room, we admired a Modern wooden sculpture that David carved himself.

Opposite:
Three generations enjoying an evening after dinner by their
fireplace. The Blocks decided to sandblast their fireplace for
a stripped down, raw look. Grooved siding, post and beam,
and large expanses of glass are all standard Eichler issue.

Adriene and David discussing the virtues of Modern living.

This rear view illustrates the concept of indoor/outdoor living.
If not for the wall of glass, the entire living room could be
regarded as a lanai.

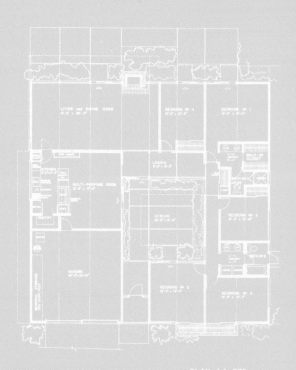

PLAN LA-375

CLAUDE OAKLAND
ARCHITECT   A.I.A.

AREA ANALYSIS
LIVING AREA   2550   Square feet
GARAGE   448   Square feet
TOTAL   3000   Square feet

Eng-Biondo Residence

John and Adriene moved to Balboa Highlands after the 1994 Northridge earthquake, figuring it was time to move from their circa 1956, three-bedroom Palmer and Krisel home in industrial Sun Valley. And though it needed a lot of work, they knew this five-bedroom classic post and beam Eichler with views of O'Melveny Park was a diamond in the rough. As you enter, you walk through a narrow passageway into the atrium. First time visitors are pleasantly surprised that they're still *outside* after opening the front door. Then you walk into the loggia which opens up into a 10-foot high living room, the back of which is a floor-to-ceiling glass curtain wall overlooking the hills. Following the 1971 Sylmar earthquake, the former owners installed a swimming pool and embarked on a Spanish Revival. Original floors had been replaced with Spanish pavers and the walls of the exterior and atrium were coated in fake rock. All of this had to be jack-hammered out, with new concrete poured and custom Eichler siding milled. A heavy, double-door wrought iron gate up front also had to go, and a new front door and entry was rebuilt from the original blueprints. But for this animation director and photographer couple, it's all been worthwhile. Model LA-375, architect Claude Oakland.

Three years after Eng and Biondo bought their
Eichler in 1995, they restored their home back to
its original Modern style and designed a Modern
concrete pattern for their atrium.

Opposite:
Again, the indoor/outdoor concept is well
illustrated by this rear view of the house, (from the
backyard looking in). The opposite view reveals
a beautiful vista of the O'Melveny Park hills. With
its flat roof and clean, linear lines, this Claude
Oakland model reflects the International Style best
of all the Eichler models.

Morritt Residence

Originally from Canada, Jeff is a designer who owns his own advertising company. As a lifelong fan of the Modern aesthetic, Jeff had admired Palm Springs Modern for many years before finding this Jones & Emmons Model AQJ-1805 in the Balboa Highlands tract. Jeff's background in design and building came in handy when he and his wife decided to serve as their own designer, contractor, and decorator. One of the things they are most proud of is the white porcelain tile floor that they installed themselves. Their Modern landscape was entirely done by Jeff and the result is a spectacular, Modern desert oasis in the heart of Granada Hills. Jeff seems to be on a winning streak. Not only is his commute a cinch (his company is in the San Fernando Valley so he doesn't even have to go over to the Hollywood side), but he gets to share his beautiful home with his wife Anne Marie and their young son Beckett.

This Jones & Emmons model includes a gabled section with flat wings on either sides. Balboa Highlands Eichlers did not originally include swimming pools, but many homeowners installed them later.

2" x 4" lath across the gabled portion of this Eichler provides shade, ventilation and relief from the San Fernando Valley's hot summers.

This view from the living room looking towards the front door illustrates the beauty of the atrium concept.

Opposite:
Homeowner Jeff Morritt had long admired the Mid-Century landscapes of Palm Springs, so he brought a little of Palm Springs to Granada Hills.

The rear of this house faces east, so each morning the living room and master bedroom are illuminated by the light of the rising sun. It's interesting to note that even with such abundance of light, most Eichler owners of the last 15 years, with the exception of the bedrooms, choose not to have blinds and/or curtains installed.

Clark-Bua Residence

Todd Clark was employed as a curator for the Petersen Car Museum at the time he began looking for a house. He and his wife Carol were living in a house in Laurel Canyon, but it wasn't Modern. When they saw this Claude Oakland Eichler Model LA-375 on Jimeno Street, they knew it was an ideal house to restore and to showcase Todd's landscape designs. Like many Case Study Architects from the *Arts & Architecture* program, Todd became his own first client. Serving as both landscape architect *and* client, he was able to use the work on his own house as a portfolio piece to start a new career. After designing a waterfall for his backyard and creating tiers along the back slope, he continued into the house, revamping the bathrooms and expanding the master bedroom. Soon every room in the house was brought up to date while retaining the spirit of the 1960s. Upon completion, Todd and Carol decided to relocate to Vancouver, Washington. Undeterred, they discovered yet another Modern house with a butterfly roof to restore all over again.

One of the original show models on Jimeno Ave.

A Claude Oakland, gabled roof model with a modified front door. The top of the original front door was angled in the same way as the roofline and awning that jutted out over the front entrance. This owner kept the awning but changed the unique shape of the original door to a conventional rectangular door.

Note the unpainted, raw block on this Claude Oakland model.

The Grossmans are the original owners from 1963 and still enjoy living in this Eichler. They told us that actress Jody Foster lived right across the street and that a photographer friend "discovered" her before the Fosters moved to Hollywood.

A prototype Eichler on Jimeno Ave. with a modified front door.

Sunrise on this east-facing Eichler off of Darla Ave. offers a gorgeous vista, and the landscaping ain't bad either.

Another original owner from 1964 lives in this prototype Eichler.

This beautiful Claude Oakland model sits on a corner lot. Orange and red doors are popular accent colors.

LAKEWOOD RAN ESTATES

long beach

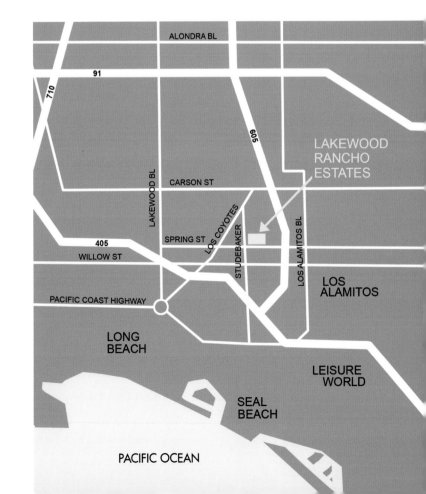

THESE DELUXE
FEATURES FOR YOU...

NEW FREEDOM GAS KITCHENS with
WESTERN-HOLLY built-in automatic gas ranges
Garbage disposals
DAY and NIGHT automatic forced air heating (70,000 BTU)
Birch kitchen cabinets with sliding doors
Built-in breakfast seats
AMCO genuine Formica fully formed sink tops
Colored rock roofs
2 FULL BATHS with colored fixtures
16' master bedroom
Double garages — attached or detached

Credits. This booklet conceived and designed by Robert Paine Advertising   Typography—Monsen

LAKEWOO

AT LAST...

WHAT YOU'VE

BEEN

LONGING FOR...

"PROGRESS
is our most important
PRODUCT"

Original brochure from the
Lakewood Rancho Estates
from 1953. Original brochure
courtesy of Doug Kramer.

RANCHO ESTATES

Sales Agents:

WALKER and LEE, Inc.

Phone: L.B. 58812

Your salesman:

Architect CHRIS CHOATE
Designer CLIFF MAY
Subdivider and Builder ROSS W. CORTESE
Sales Agents WALKER and LEE, INC.

CITY COLLEGE
Carson St.
DOUGLAS PLANT
STADIUM
SCHOOL
Spring St.
Willow St.
Stearns St.
JR. HIGH
GRAMMAR SCHOOL
Bellflower Blvd.
Palo Verde Ave.
Studebaker Rd.
Lakewood Blvd.
SHOPPING →
RANCHO LOS ALAMITOS
PARK
Los Coyotes Diagonal
Future Sepulveda Parkway
Atherton St.
Pacific Coast Highway
STATE COLLEGE

east corner of Spring Street and Palo Verde Avenue, only 3 blocks from Lakewood Rancho Estates. Here you will have access to a large market, a drug store, variety store, women's and men's apparel shops, specialty shops, and service shops...including beauty parlor, barber shop, shoe shop, etc. In addition there is enough parking space for everyone.

LAKEWOOD RANCHO ESTATES
Tract: THE CALIFORNIAN
Builder: ROSS W. CORTESE
Architect: CHRIS CHOATE
Designer: CLIFF MAY
Location: LONG BEACH, CA
Year: 1953-54

Cliff May is one of the most highly regarded Southern California architects and the "Father of Western Ranch Style." As a young man growing up in San Diego, his mother was born into an Early Spanish Californian family who owned a historic adobe. Inspired by the Early California ranches, he began designing his own distinctive ranch style homes. His rambling single story homes are oriented towards the rear of the property and views beyond, presenting a plain facade to the street. Building around a central patio or courtyard, May incorporated natural materials in cabinetry, planters, walls and fences for an earthy yet Modern look. During the 1940s, May began to move away from the heavy Early California look of wrought iron and tile and towards lightweight building materials, finishes, and transparent glass sliding doors. Though he was a building designer, Cliff May never officially became an architect, instead he worked with partner Chris Choate, who provided the necessary license. Later in his career, May was presented with an honorary AIA for his architectural achievements. A brilliantly talented man with a tremendous sense of humor, music was apparently Cliff May's first love. Flying a plane (with his own personalized "MAYDAY" license plate), the story goes that he would bring along his saxophone to entertain guests, and even had a special lightweight piano installed so he could play while he flew the plane. Cliff May's legendary body of architectural work includes thousands of tract homes and more than 1,000 custom residences throughout the U.S.

DESIGNS

Architectural rendering of Plan 4A, a four-bedroom model.

Opposite, from top:
Designer Cliff May (center) with his architect partner Chris Choate and builder Ross W. Cortese discussing their Lakewood Rancho Estates project.

Aerial view of the Lakewood Tract.

Original rendering of Plan C, a three-bedroom model.

It is always a pleasure to visit the Ranchos. Though nearly four miles from the ocean, the friendly, beach vibe here gives the community a relaxed Southern California feel. The Ranchos are Cliff May's largest tract and were built in four phases between 1953-54 by subdivider and developer Ross W. Cortese as part of a larger Cliff May development in Lakewood. Creative homeowners in every field from architecture and graphic design to French cooking are doing fabulous things with their Modern ranch-style homes. Realtors Doug and Rochelle Kramer can recall when "Even realtors didn't want to deal with the Ranchos," as Rochelle explained. The couple are key to the tract's renaissance and are overjoyed about the positive activity. Seeing the smiles and young families strolling through the neighborhood, you can certainly feel the sense of community.

The Ranchos are one-story post and beam homes with attached or detached double car garages. Homeowners appreciate the easy flow from inside to out, which gives the homes an openness that feels much larger than the original 1,130 to 1,600 square feet. Homes can be L-shaped, and either attached to garages or carports, or set slightly back, opening onto courtyards through floor-to-ceiling doors. Fences provide privacy and increase the usable space of the house. There are six basic models with three or four bedrooms, including a Lanai model with a passageway that opens into the courtyard. The houses are built on five foot modules, making each half of a pair of French doors two and a half feet wide. Original interiors feature genuine birch cabinetry with built-in "Jack and Jill" wardrobes in the bedrooms and all-Modern kitchens with Western-Holly appliances.

65

Burke Residence

Robert Burke is an elementary school principal who moved into the Rancho Estates from West Hollywood. Robert's home is set into a lush oasis with a stunning subtropical garden, which provides privacy around a large swimming pool. He has taken great pains to keep his restoration true to the original spirit, even replacing aluminum sliding doors with an original set that was discarded at the curb by another homeowner. Although he says it's rare, you can still come across lucky finds like birch cabinets, doors with intact windows, and other original accessories. "I love the light. I love the lines," Robert says of his Rancho. "They're very smartly designed."

Opposite:
Magic hour at the Burke Residence. The kidney-shaped pool was installed after the house was built, but in keeping with the Modern style.

From top:
Expansive walls of glass are a common feature of a Cliff May design.

Burke renovated his original terrazzo step-in shower with new plumbing and glass tiles.

Kight Residence

Greg and Anna-Karin are committed to staying "green" while making the most of their Californian Ranch home. A practicing architect with a keen eye for efficiency, Greg and his wife have custom tailored their living space to suit their lifestyle—clean, bright and simple. A cabinet houses an integrated state-of-the-art washer/dryer that is one single, space-saving appliance. Wherever possible the Kights have maximized their layout and introduced Modern furnishings that they have adapted for the highest and best use.

Opposite:
Clean and simple, the Kights enjoy their living space while the house undergoes renovation.

The renovation includes new cabinets and laminate-covered plywood countertops.

The Kights selected a highly efficient washer/dryer combo hidden inside a cabinet out of sight.

Russell Residence

Roger Russell is a marketing director at Quicksilver, a retail shop for surf and skate-wear. He and his wife Casey invested five months getting their home ready before moving in. In order to give themselves and their pit bull Bella more living area, they opened up the kitchen and relocated the washer and dryer to the garage. They also installed ceiling insulation. After removing the old linoleum flooring, they decided to polish the concrete slab. "It can take diamond polishing like marble or terrazzo," Casey told us, "so we polished it until it turned a silvery-gray." Displaying their art is a little more of a challenge, with all the glass window-walls, but Casey pointed out that each home is unique and completely private since they are set back from the street.

Opposite:
This picture from the original brochure shows a patio with a built-in fire pit.

The Russells used commercially available concrete blocks to create a complementary pattern in their courtyard.

Here the original footprint of the Cliff May design is maintained while contemporary elements like a polished slab floor, new kitchen cabinets, and appliances have replaced the old and tired ones.

The reverse angle shows how the layout, or "footprint," of the kitchen, family room, and living room have been left unchanged. Skylights and cabinets are all new.

Inside the house, the light play in the late afternoon is beautiful to watch.

Modern ranch homes are surprisingly receptive to a wide variety of eclectic furniture and decorations. Here, in Stamps' office, his surfboard collection and industrial office desk are not at all out of place.

Opposite:
The Stamps are not locked to one specific style or period but use a mixture of traditional, hi-tech, Modern, and surf culture elements to create an environment that suits them. This is totally in keeping with Cliff May's approach to design, where Spanish Revival elements and furnishings decorate his Western Ranch homes.

Stamps Residence

Tim and Linda Stamps moved to the Ranchos from their rented beach bungalow in nearby Seal Beach. "That's where I grew up," Tim says, "I'm a surfer, and I really didn't want to leave the beach." But since he and Linda wanted to invest in a home, they searched in Long Beach and found exactly what they were looking for at the Cliff May Ranchos. "We feel like we're on vacation," Linda says. "It's so open. It feels like Hawaii or Palm Springs." Tim designs and builds surfboards, so he handcrafted the replacement cabinetry in their home, carefully matching the original birch. Tim is fascinated by the parallel between surfboard design and their Cliff May home. "The houses have a great, simple design that's really functional like a surfboard. There's not a lot of wasted space. It's simple utility that's beautiful in its simplicity."

Clifford Residence

After falling in love with Mid-Century Modern Palm Springs, Steve and Sandi Clifford decided it was time to leave their Spanish Colonial home and Go Modern. And as soon as they found RanchoStyle.com, it wasn't long before they were living their dream. Sandi is a 7th grade teacher and her husband Steve an English professor at Cerritos College. The couple purchased their home in 2006, originally a four-bedroom model built in 1954 during the tract's last phase of development. As a former owner had expanded the living room, the Cliffords envisioned a wall of gorgeous built-in birch cabinetry in the original style, so they hired local craftsman Joe Estrada to design it for them. In the kitchen they installed Ann Sacks' "Starburst" ceramic tiles designed by Barbara Barry. Steve, Sandi, and their dogs Sassy and Ella seem to be thoroughly enjoying their new Modern lifestyle. Sandi says their home is remarkably livable: "We use every room, every day."

We have visited many Modern homes and often are greeted by Polynesian elements such as Tiki heads. Here, a modest sized Tiki head can be seen peeking out of the bushes next to the patio chairs.

The Cliffords used new decorative tiles against the back kitchen wall. Custom cabinets were fabricated by local carpenter Joe Estrada, who works on many Cliff May homes in the area.

Johnson Residence

Merritt Johnson moved from a condo in Marina del Rey to her 1953 Rancho in 2008. She decorated her home in a Modern beach bungalow style, which complements the original tongue-and-groove ceilings, push-out windows, translucent MistLight glass, and Jack and Jill wardrobe closets. Merritt personalized her property with sustainable xeriscape landscaping designed by C-Arc, which includes a firepit and conversation seating and custom front and rear fencing for privacy. A mechanical engineer for General Motors, Merritt is also a competitive swimmer who swims daily at Los Alamitos Bay and Cal State Long Beach. She shares her home with Rusty, a German shepherd mix, and Fo, a military macaw native to South America.

Opposite:
To Merritt's macaw, Modern living is just as natural as the rain forest.

The door/wall from the master bedroom to the outside is often left open. Note the level from the interior to the exterior is the same, thus minimizing the difference between the inside and the outside.

Here, Merritt tries to keep her dog Rusty motionless for a 10 second exposure.

LIVING-CONDIT HOMES

IONED

northridge

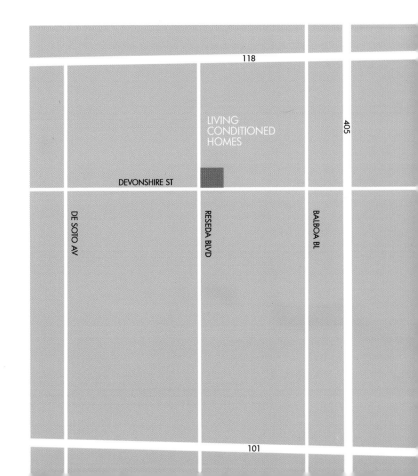

118

405

LIVING
CONDITIONED
HOMES

DEVONSHIRE ST

DE SOTO AV

RESEDA BLVD

BALBOA BL

101

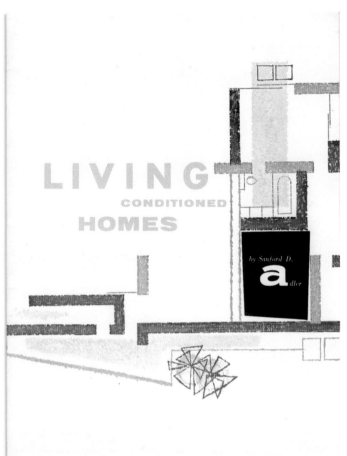

Sanford D. Adler's Living-Conditioned Homes. Original brochure courtesy Mark Noland.

A Personal Message
from the Builder

It is my pleasure to welcome you to our "Living-Conditioned" homes in Northridge. In these fine homes we offer our concept of the theme of National Home Week — "Better Homes for Better Living." Among the original ideas presented in these homes, we are sure you will find many features that will hold special interest for you — perhaps even some that you may not have realized you wanted.

The Valley's Northridge "Living-Conditioned" homes were designed to fulfill present and future requirements of comfortable, luxurious living. Important living-conditioning features were skillfully coordinated in the "Living-Conditioned" homes to provide families with the greatest degree of comfort, livability and convenience.

We believe that the Northridge "Living-Conditioned" homes set the pace for all that is convenient, advanced, and comfortable in modern living.

So we invite you to take a "forward look" into tomorrow's living today!

The homes are open for your inspection from 10 a.m. to 9 p.m. daily.

We hope that you will take time to look around, enjoy yourself, ask questions, and make yourself at home.

Cordially,

Sanford D. Adler

Sanford D. Adler

**LOOK AHEAD
PLAN AHEAD
STAY AHEAD!**
with a Sanford D. Adler-built
"Living-Conditioned" Home

LIVING-CONDITIONED HOMES
Builder: SANFORD D. ADLER
Architects: PALMER AND KRISEL
Engineers and Land Planners: VOORHEIS-TRINDLE CO.
Location: NORTHRIDGE, CA
Year: 1957

"We believe that Northridge 'Living-Conditioned' homes sets the pace for all that is convenient, advanced and comfortable in modern living…so we invite you to take a 'forward look' into tomorrow's living today!"

—Living-Conditioned Homes brochure, 1957

Sanford D. Adler built many subdivisions in the San Fernando Valley in the 1950s. Here, he paired up with the architectural team of Palmer and Krisel, A.I.A. These Modern homes boasted of *acoustical planning* that was sound-conditioned for reduced noise, and *light conditioned* for maximum light with minimum glare and shadows. Color consultant Doris Palmer created an atmosphere of harmonious colors that complemented the architecture and landscape. Interior furnishings by Albert Parvin Co. were included as an option. Living-Conditioned Homes featured five floor plans and 17 exterior styles, starting from $24,750. Post and beam houses are constructed with solid plank roofs and concrete slab floors covered in vinyl asbestos and pure vinyl tiles. Glass windows with aluminum sashes run the length of the rear of the homes. Adler's brochure describes the lanai as "a storage area which affords 90 square feet of space." Some utilized this area as an extension of the living room, entertaining weekend guests and families with outdoor parties and barbecues, in the classic style of indoor/outdoor living.

An all-electric kitchen included appliances from Westinghouse listed as "electric servants to lighten household tasks. The Westinghouse deluxe 24-inch electric oven and range, with ventilating fan and Nutone built-in food center, Westinghouse dishwasher and disposer handle daily household routine with ease and efficiency."

The Living-Conditioned Homes tract is located towards the northern end of the San Fernando Valley, south of the Santa Susana Mountains and within walking distance of Cal State Northridge.

Carrillo Residence

Alex Carrillo's home is a stunning Modern design with a dramatic cinder block wall that runs the entire length of the living room, continuing through the window wall and out to the back patio. An art instructor at Cal State Northridge, Carrillo's art and the original works of many other artists are displayed on the walls. Setting the mood at the front entry is a mixed-medium piece entitled *The Four Seasons* designed by Carrillo in 1955. He tells how back in 1957 he opened the front door for the very first time and stepping into the entry realized his art had finally found its home. Here, *The Four Seasons* is showcased perfectly, backlit on both sides just as Carrillo envisioned it. In the kitchen, the overhead cabinet is a transparent floating box with sliding reeded glass doors. Its accessibility to the dining area makes serving guests a pleasure. Nearly every room is original right down to a His n' Hers wardrobe cube in the master bedroom. Carrillo's backyard garden of wildflowers was teeming with butterflies and hummingbirds when he toured us through. Adjacent to the garden is a working art studio, which Carrillo had custom designed to complement the home's architecture. High ceilings and clerestory windows create a bright work space with plenty of storage and display areas.

Opposite:
This mixed-media art piece by Carrillo was done *before* he found his Living-Conditioned house. In fact, it helped the Carrillos to identify their dream home. Like the prince in Cinderella, who searched for his soulmate by finding the person that fit the slipper, Alex knew that the Palmer & Krisel house was "the one" when his sculpture fit the house like a glove. He is the home's first and only owner.

Alex sipping tea while contemplating his options for his back yard garden.

Alex and Adriene talk about what attracted him to the house. Aside from the fact that it was close to Cal State Northridge, where he teaches art, he loved the open plan and with the addition of his studio done by the same design firm, he ran out of reasons not to buy it. He's been happy with his decision ever since.

Alex and his beautiful wife shortly after they moved into the neighborhood.

Opposite, from top:
Now in his 80s, Alex is down-sizing and giving many of his original sketches to friends. This custom built studio served him for over 50 years. Clerestory windows allow sunlight to pour in during the day and the high ceiling gives a feeling of a much larger space.

Original Carrillo sculptures can be found throughout his home and studio.

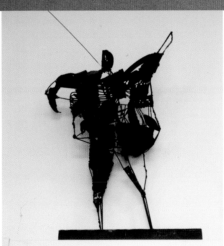

Original hallway light fixture still in use.

Original owners, Chris and Marian, kicking off the dust on the transistors of this vintage Thomas organ.

Amazingly, this original starburst light fixture (also known as a "dingbat") came with the house and is still in use today.

Opposite:
When compared to the artist's rendering, the exterior of this house appears almost completely intact.

This rendering can be found in the original brochure.

Christy Residence

Chris and Marian Christy are a rare couple. Original owners who have lived in their home since 1957, they have raised a family and yet maintain their home with nearly all the original features it came with, right down to the floor tile and countertops. When we asked why they have never remodeled or changed a fixture, they told us, "We like our home just the way we found it." And looking around at the intact kitchen, baths, even the sputnik wall sconce...we believe them. The day we stopped by, Chris, a former electronics salesman, was happy to chip a few golf balls on the Bermuda grass that seems to go for miles across the Christy's backyard. Only in Southern California.

Noland Residence

The Noland family relocated from Portland four years ago when they discovered their Southern California dream home online. Now Mark is working in computer graphics for Autodesk in Venice. Mark and Gemma's home features a "butterfly" roof, one of the iconic signatures of Palmer and Krisel. The spacious, open plan expands the family living space by allowing the living room, family room, kitchen, and terrace to run lengthwise across the rear of the house, opening onto one another. A flagstone fireplace and hearth is ideal for entertaining, especially when Mark is mixing flaming Polynesian drinks in his Bamboo Bar. Gemma does professional baking in true 50's style in an exceptionally original kitchen. Circa 1957 features include charcoal gray tile countertops, Westinghouse built-ins, a mixing center, in-wall clock, and cabinetry with perforated masonite doors. The Noland Residence is pending historic status.

C2

Architect Bill Krisel is well known for the use of the "butterfly roof" design. A previous owner enclosed the carport in order to create a garage. Aside from this modification, the clerestory windows and rock wall are unchanged.

This rendering and C2 plan appeared in the brochure given out to prospective home buyers in 1957.

Gemma Noland and daughter Frances in their Modern Tiki-fied living room. The Bamboo Bar that Mark built is the first thing visitors see after entering the house.

A sculpture that belonged to the former owner, who was an executive for Witco, the premiere company that produced sculptures and wood art during the 1950s and 1960s.

The Witco piece to the right of the fireplace also belonged to the former owner.

From top:
The original doorknob still in use on the front door.

In-wall kitchen clocks like this one were standard in this tract.

This trio of wall lights also came with the house.

Opposite, from top:
The Nolands are very happy with the degree of authenticity this house came with, especially the kitchen.

In the brochure, these Westinghouse appliances were sale features.

As a baker and cook, Gemma uses these electric appliances almost every day.

A PLAN

A1

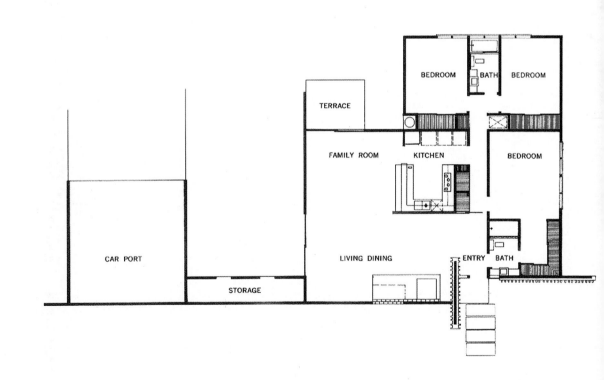

B1

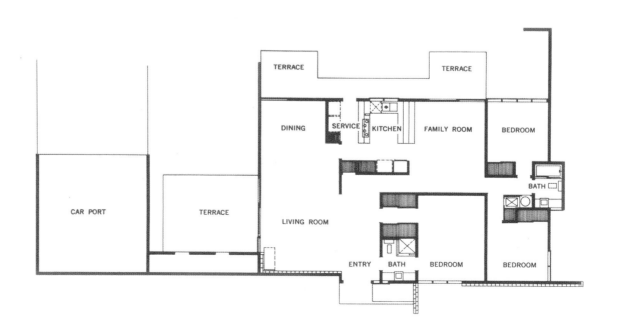

MAR VISTA HOU

SING

mar vista

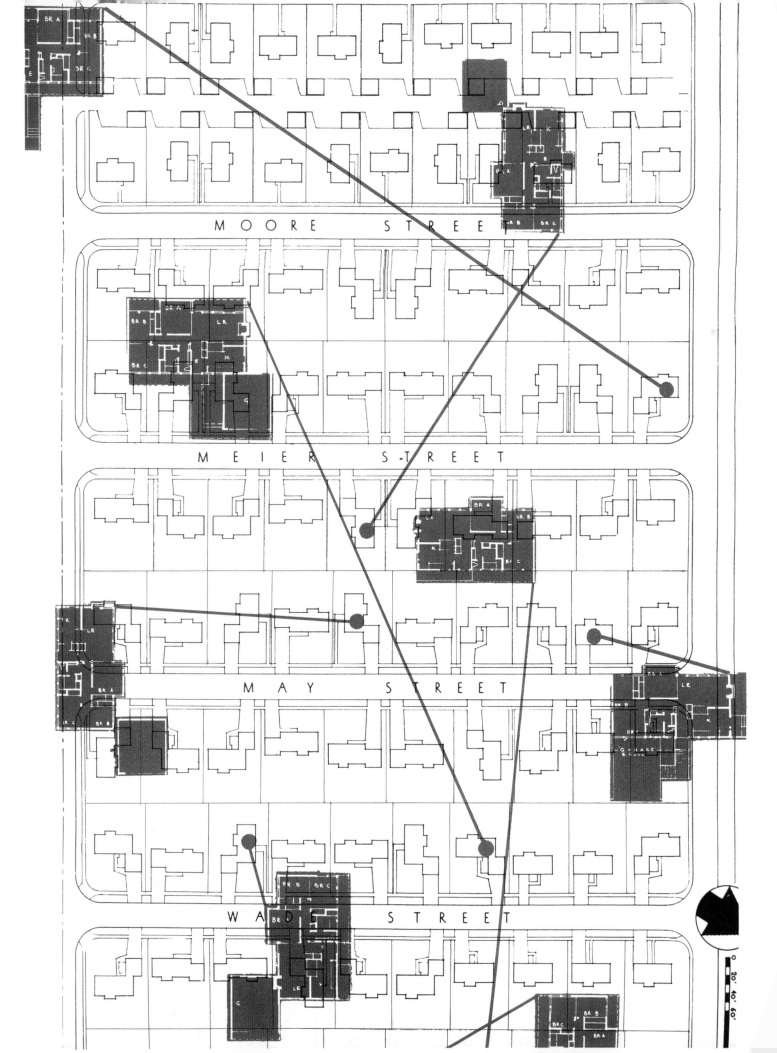

MOORE STREET

MEIER STREET

MAY STREET

WADE STREET

MAR VISTA HOUSING

Tract: MODERNIQUE HOMES
Builder: MAR VISTA HOUSING DEVELOPMENT
Architects: GREGORY AIN, JOSEPH JOHSON, &
ALFRED DAY
Landscape Architect: GARRETT ECKBO
Construction by: ADVANCE DEVELOPMENT CO.
Location: MAR VISTA, CA
Year: 1948

It's not every day that you come across a virtually intact Modernist tract of architectural homes, complete with Modern landscaping by Garrett Eckbo. Here in the Mar Vista tract of "Modernique" (Modern + Unique) Homes, architect Gregory Ain created one of the very first Modernist residential tracts. Fiercely guarded by loyal homeowners, the Moderniques are also officially protected by a Historic Preservation Overlay Zone. Mar Vista was the first postwar development in Los Angeles to be granted such a historic district designation by the City of Los Angeles.

Located on Los Angeles' Westside, near Los Angeles International Airport, Mar Vista was originally bordered by aircraft industry giants such as Douglas Aircraft and Hughes Aircraft. As Southern California grew into a hub for the aerospace industry during World War II, mass housing was constructed at an accelerated rate to accommodate wartime workers. The Gregory Ain Vista Tract (Mar Vista Housing) subdivision was proposed by the Advance Development Co. and designed as a collaborative effort. The development began soon after it was subdivided in 1946 with all the houses constructed during 1948.

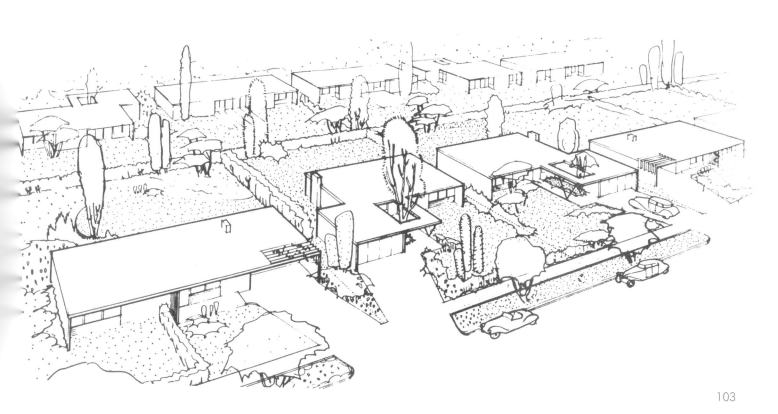

Gregory Ain designed the Modernique homes in a Postwar Modern style with partners Joseph Johnson and Alfred Day. Houses were constructed of prefabricated materials, utilizing state-of-the-art systems and techniques. As Ain's interest was in designing socially conscious housing, he focused on creating a livable community that would encourage friendly interaction between neighbors. Unfortunately, the Federal Housing Administration would not finance a racially integrated neighborhood, so only 52 homes were completed.

Eight variations on a single floor plan were designed, with the modest homes averaging 1,050 square feet. The homes are flat-roofed dwellings with V-shaped pipe supports that distinguish the front elevations. Convertible interior spaces can be divided by sliding panels, pocket doors, and blinds. Custom built-ins meant new homeowners could move right in without having to worry about investing in new furnishings. And tying the community landscape design together was innovative landscape architect Garrett Eckbo. With the exception of the Model House, rear yards were left to the homeowner to landscape. In 1948, the homes sold for $12,000, which was considered relatively expensive at the time. In 1950, a house was built from one of Ain's plans and exhibited inside the courtyard at the Museum of Modern Art, New York.

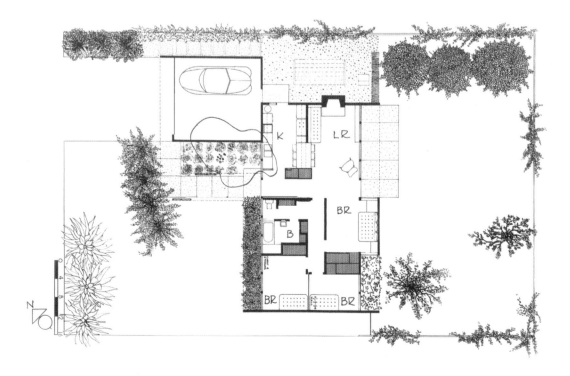

BASIC DWELLING TYPE A

The Mar Vista Tract is the result of Total Design, from the interior color detail, layout, and choice of exterior colors, to the overall community planning and landscaping. In contrast to the conservative exterior paint choices we see today, Modernique homes were not painted off-white or beige. Buyers were offered 23 different color design combinations created especially for their unique Modernist home.

Hans and Amanda telling Adriene how they
managed to keep most of their kitchen intact and
how much they admire the thinking behind the
Gregory Ain design.

The couple decorated their dining room with
European Art Deco furniture which works
fabulously in these houses.

Adamson-Seward Residence

Hans Adamson and Amanda Seward's home possesses many of the original design features that characterize a Modernique home. Though the living room has been expanded, an original folding door opens to become a wall. In the kitchen, a horizontal Venetian blind can be opened or closed to act as a divider. Hans also designed a low, wooden cabinet that serves as both storage and room divider and blends seamlessly into the design of the house. He also custom crafted a Modern side gate to match their home's distinctive character. Amanda and Hans are committed to preserving their Modernique home and neighborhood. An entertainment attorney, Amanda initiated the movement to create a historic district and Hans served on the board and created a comprehensive Mar Vista Homes website. An accomplished musician, Hans also designs electronic sound systems for the music industry. They live in a Type 2, Style 2Lt Modernique.

Opposite:
Subtropical plants seem to love this location just a few miles from the Pacific Ocean. The exterior metal gate was designed by Hans, who was inspired by a gate he had seen in a vintage architecture book.

The folding wall design created a modular approach to the usable space. Depending upon what is desired, larger rooms can be sectioned off and smaller spaces created.

Jones Residence

A stunningly original example, Bonnie's Modernique home is often used for location filming. On one of the days we visited, a Goodyear commercial was being filmed in front of her home. Meier Street retains original plantings of Magnolia trees along the parkway. The walkway canopy to the home is supported by V-shaped pipe supports and is a lovely lead-in to the front entry. This Type 1, Style 1Lcw residence is built parallel to the street with the garage attached diagonally.

It's easy to imagine yourself here in 1948 since just about nothing has changed, including Ain's signature V-shaped pipe supports.

Major-Vaquette Residence

One of the best modified examples, Les and Pascale's home is a Type 1, Style 1L Modernique. Pastel colors and finishes and subtropical plantings work together to give their home an open, Southern California feel. They've also outfitted their kitchen with a retro style Big Chill refrigerator and other appliances that give any visitor a portal to the past.

In order to create a library and study, the
living room was expanded with a raised
ceiling and a rear entrance.

Woodruff-Dubrobich Residence

This Modernique home features a unique library addition designed by the local architectural firm Daly Genik Architects. According to Kevin Daly, the intent was to "build in a way that was compatible with the existing building (which had been unsympathetically altered over the years) but would not mimic the original building. The low scale of the original building made it so we could get a large vertical change of scale without making the new part too tall." Sliding glass door panels lead outdoors to a new patio and garden with a reflecting pool designed by Garrett Eckbo in his last professional commission. After more than half a century, Eckbo returned to the community he had originally designed back in 1948.

A sliding glass door leads to the lovely outdoor patio designed by Garrett Eckbo. This was the landscape master's last project.

The northwest corner of the library showing the panels opening to the outdoors.

A custom gate in the neighborhood.

MUTUAL HOUSI
ASSOCIATIATES

NG

INC.

brentwood

BLUEPRINT FOR
CALIFORNIA LIVING
CRESTWOOD HILLS

LIVE IN THE COMMUNITY OF TOMORROW...TODAY

Original brochure courtesy
Jon and Kathy Leader.

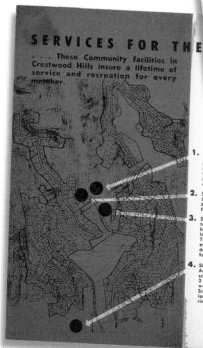

SERVICES FOR THE

... These Community facilities in Crestwood Hills insure a lifetime of service and recreation for every member.

1. **PLAYGROUNDS** — A 7 acre area set aside for a playground will be maintained as a public park and sports center under agreement between M.H.A. and the City of Los Angeles.

2. **STORES, SHOPS** — Plans have been developed for a complete shopping center within the community.

3. **SOCIAL CENTERS** — An auditorium, nursery school and hobby center will be maintained by Crestwood Hills. There'll be recreation for everyone in social gatherings, dances, parties, leisure-time handicrafts.

4. **SCHOOLS** — The City of Los Angeles is to build a primary school on Kenter Ave., just 3 minutes' walk from Crestwood Hills. Junior High School and High School are located at Texas and Barrington.

Members of M.H.A. subscribe $2,000 upon their application for a homesite in Crestwood Hills. Once a site is selected, any difference between the $2,000 subscription and the purchase price of the lot is payable in three monthly installments.

MEMBERSHIP IN M.H.A.—

Membership in M.H.A. is open to anyone who subscribes to its principles and aims and whose application is approved by the Association's board of directors. To be admitted to active membership (with immediate eligibility for a Crestwood Hills homesite) applications are accepted upon the payment of $525 which represents a deposit against the $2,000 subscription and $25 membership fee.

MUTUAL HOUSING ASSOCIATES, INC.
Tract: CRESTWOOD HILLS
Builder: MUTUAL HOUSING ASSOCIATES INC.
Architects: WHITNEY SMITH, A. QUINCY JONES, & EDGARDO CONTINI with JAMES CHARLTON & WAYNE WILLIAMS
Location: BRENTWOOD, CA
Year: 1950

From smallest to largest, all homes have the same modern styling: expanses of glass, sweeping views, natural wood interiors, engineered storage space, built-in furniture, convenient living-dining arrangements, rooms that combine with outdoor terraces, and kitchens that housewives dream about.

THE HOUSEWIFE REIGNS—

Work on the first 200 homes in Crestwood Hills is under way. Construction of 200 additional homes will begin on completion of the first group. M.H.A. has 25 individual home plans to meet the varying tastes, needs and pocketbooks of its members. Homes range in cost from $8500 to $25,000.

The homemaker's voice has been heard in Crestwood Hills. M.H.A.'s members were polled for their likes and dislikes in home design before plans were drawn. Crestwood Hills families won't have to fit themselves into their homes. These homes are fitted to their families.

Community assets in Crestwood Hills—parks, playgrounds, social centers, etc.—are held jointly by the residents. Homes and lots are individually owned. Lots are deeded to owners on completion of homes.

Homesites range in cost from $2,000 to $5,500. Lots in nearby subdivisions cost $6,000 to $15,000.

Cost of all improvements, sewers, paving, drains, gas and electricity—is included in the cost of the lot. Crestwood Hills is approved by the Federal Housing Administration. Conservative appraisers have put loan valuations on these homesites at more than their cost to members.

designs for living

IF YOU WANT TO KNOW MORE ABOUT CRESTWOOD HILLS—

Drive to Crestwood Hills. Look over this beautiful site — you'll be welcome. Access: Sunset Blvd., to Kenter Ave.: turn north on Kenter to Hanley to the site. Members of M.H.A. are at the Administration Bldg. on Sundays or— Telephone the office of M.H.A. (BRadshaw 2-4159). Ask for an interview with a member of M.H.A. who can answer your questions and help you apply for membership if you wish.

IF YOU LIVE EAST OR NORTHEAST

in Los Angeles and want a quick look at a typical Crestwood Hills home, see the three-bedroom home built by M.H.A.'s architects at 753 Rome Drive, on Mt. Washington. Access: Figueroa or Arroyo Seco to W. Avenue 45, uphill to Rome Drive.

CRESTWOOD HILLS
co-operative project
of the
MUTUAL HOUSING ASSOCIATION, INC
a non-profit corporation
626 No. Robertson Boulevard
Los Angeles 46, California

123

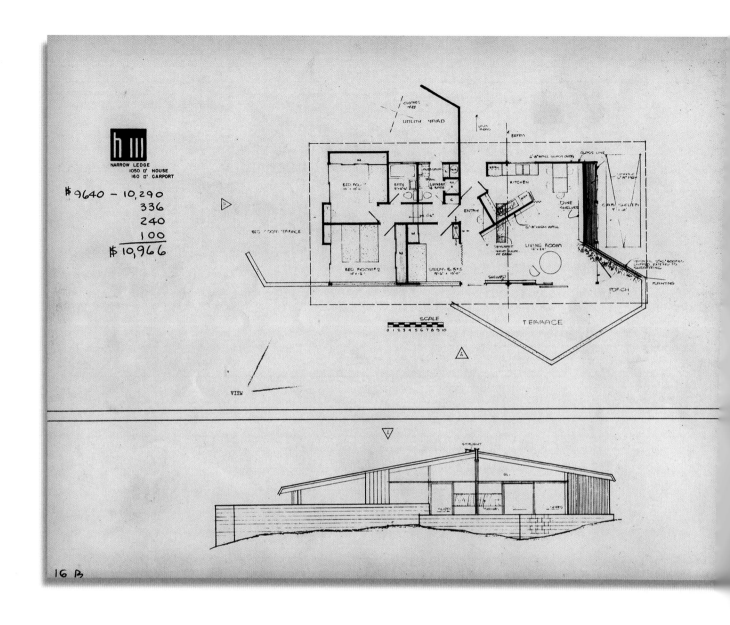

After WW II, Ray Siegel met up with three of his studio musician friends, Leonard Krupnick, Jules Sulkan, and Gene Komer, to talk about forming a cooperative in order to build homes for their families. Their idea was that by pooling their resources, they could get more bang for their buck. It quickly expanded when they placed an ad in the *Los Angeles Times* and 400 interested parties responded. Purchasing 800 acres in an area in the Santa Monica Mountains known as Crestwood Hills, they interviewed numerous architects including Richard Neutra. Initially they hired architects A. Quincy Jones, Whitney R. Smith, and Jones' former employer, Douglas Honnold. Other architects including John Lautner and Francis Lockwood, engineer Edgardo Contini, and landscape architect Garrett Eckbo were also involved. Eventually Honnold had to bow out. And former Taliesin apprentices, architects Jim Charlton and Wayne Williams worked as draftsmen. Even though this site is situated in the hills, they minimized bulldozing and damage to the landscape. Their designs were environmentally sensitive when none of the other developers were at the time. In addition to individual homes, parks, a nursery school, gas station, and grocery store were considered as part of this development which became known as the Mutual Housing Association (MHA).

Two major requirements dictate the form of this dwelling: to organize a structure for erection on a narrow ledge occurring on the downhill side of the road; to create a minimum three bedroom, 2 bath house.

The building rests on a terraced slab and lies under a double sloping roof. The major axis is oriented toward the view.

A skylighted entrance extends welcome to the visitor; offers a glimpse of the view terrace; and acts as the hub of pedestrian circulation. Ushering from this central space in one direction are the quiet areas and in another direction, the social areas. Down 1' - 6" from the social space are two bedrooms and a bath; each bedroom expands to a private terrace. In the same zone, but at the upper level, are a study-bedroom and a half bath.

The social area is composed to offer maximum flexibility. Physical expansion to a view terrace makes the living spaces visually spacious.

BASIC MATERIALS: Slab floor - two levels. 1' - 6" difference. Plywood, redwood boards, glass, concrete block walls. Exposed plank and beam ceiling, color in stain.

ENTRY: Guest coat storage adjacent. Screened from direct view from living room. Skylight over.

KITCHEN: Screened from living room by storage cabinets. May be completely closed off by sliding doors. Exhaust fan over range. Washable walls. Special floor surface.

DINING AREA: Alcove near kitchen and social area may be screened from living room by curtain.

LIVING AREA: Has built-in book storage. Expands to covered porch and view terrace.

BATH-UTILITY: Combines bath with laundry tray and space for automatic washer. Washable walls. Special floor surface.

BEDROOM NO. 1: Bunk beds. Generous storage. Door opens to terrace.

BEDROOM NO. 2: Twin bed space. Windows on two sides. Door to terrace.

STUDY-BEDROOM: Flexible use room. May serve as study, guest room or bed room.

CARPORT: Shelter is provided for a single car with storage cabinet adjacent.

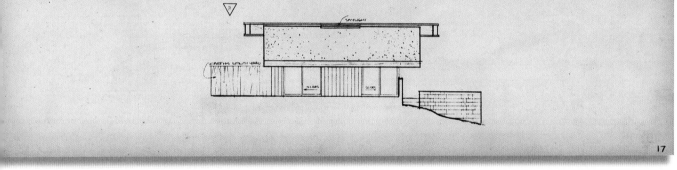

17

The overwhelming crowd that responded to an ad in the paper was unexpected.

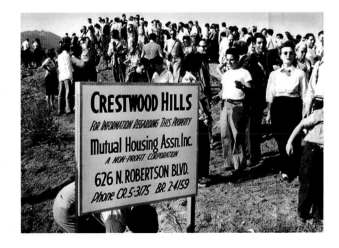

Apparently only happy faces were seen.

A private driveway leading up to the Buckner house on top of a bluff shows the area's hilly topography.

Opposite:
Note the understated black linoleum floor tiles and original built-in cabinetry.

Mutual Housing Association Site Office

Not only is Cory Buckner an architect, but she is also a writer, historian, and preservationist. She and her husband, architect and professor Nick Roberts, moved to Crestwood Hills in 1994. Here, they practice what they preach by living in the Mutual Housing's original site office, a Modernist tour de force. In order to preserve Crestwood's unique homes, where only 33 of the original MHA homes remain intact, Cory has spearheaded the movement to protect them by landmarking them, one by one. So far, 16 of the homes have been officially designated as Historic-Cultural Monuments, including the MHA Site Office (HCM No. 680) and the Sherwood Residence, which they also own (HCM No. 698). In 2002, Cory Buckner's book on the work of A. Quincy Jones was published.

Just before you reach the house, an amoeba-shaped pool dares you to jump in.

From the inside looking out, the split-level roof is evident. Double angled beams pierce the overhead soffit.

Schott House

Living in a modest Model h702X, Jon and Kathy Leader needed more space for their growing family, which included a daughter, a son, and a Cocker Spaniel. In a sensitive expansion by Cory Buckner, they have retained all the original features of this post and beam house with a floor-to-ceiling glass wall at the rear, concrete block fireplace, vertical blind/partition wall, and split-level kitchen and living room. Views from the backyard towards the canyon are incredible as the light and shadow dance throughout the day. The renovation included an expansion of the kitchen/dining room as well as adding a pool, which is hidden from the street. Thanks to the Leaders, neighborhood concerts have returned to Crestwood Hills Park. Originally owned by well-to-do pharmacist Herman Schott, the home was designated Historic-Cultural Monument No. 682 in 2000.

Opposite:
Architect Cory Buckner helped the
Leaders expand their home while keeping
the spirit of the original design.

Notice the use of natural light in this late
afternoon scene. The architect's goal was
to keep the natural setting as much as
possible and use split levels throughout.

Kathy and Jon Leader with their daughter Jessica
in their beautiful living room. The vertical louvers
next to the fireplace are a modular idea similar to
the folding walls found in the Mar Vista tract. It's
closed in this picture, but when opened, allows
the flow of one room into the next, opening the
space dramatically. The Leaders eclectic taste
in art combines African sculptures with Modern
Barcelona chairs...and it all works.

Concrete block design of their original fireplace.
This is where the front half of the house drops
down into the living room and backyard, keeping
the elevation changes of the original lot.

Israel House

A remarkable survivor of the devastating 1961 Brentwood fire, this is a home that is as dramatic as it is livable. Steps from the carport lead into the lower level of this Model h105 home. Douglas fir plywood interiors and a custom brick fireplace lend a warmth and mountain chalet feel. The master bedroom opens onto a serene garden, and a second bedroom functions as a library and music room for owner Dianne Phillips, who lives and works out of her hillside home. The Israel House is protected as a Historic-Cultural Monument, No. 693.

The front entrance to the Philips house. Note the asymmetrical angle of the roof.

As in many of Frank Lloyd Wright's homes, you entered a low ceiling loggia area upon entering the front door. This would then open into a much larger space with a higher ceiling and serves as an introduction to the space.

Opposite:
The angled ceiling and wall of glass in the master bedroom give you a sense of expansive space seldom found in conventional homes.

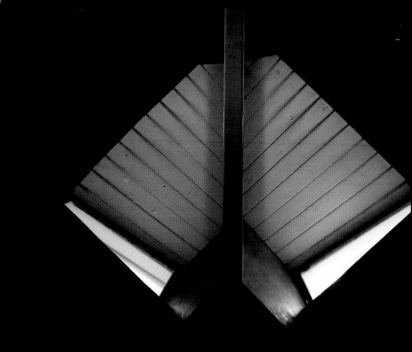

The living room upstairs offers a terrific view of Kenter Canyon. Many people think of Modern homes as cold, sterile places, but the Crestwood tract is constructed from natural wood and brick, which creates an organic, welcoming environment.

The clerestory window above the master bath acts like a skylight letting in natural light.

This corner sink is a brilliant use of space with an excellent flair for design, functional yet attractive.

Bibliography

Books

Adamson, Paul, and compiled by Marty Arbunich. *Eichler: Modernism Rebuilds the American Dream* (Layton: Gibbs Smith, 2002).

Buckner, Cory. *A. Quincy Jones.* (New York: Phaidon Press, Inc., 2002).

Chase, John. *Glitter Stucco & Dumpster Diving.* (New York and London: Verso, 2000).

Cygelman, Adele. *Palm Springs Modern.* (New York: Rizzoli International Publications, 1999).

Eckbo, Garrett. *Landscape for Living.* (New York: Duell, Sloan & Pearce, 1950).

Editors of Architectural Record. *The Treasury of Contemporary Houses.* (New York: F.W. Dodge, 1954).

Editors of Architectural Record. *The Second Treasury of Contemporary Houses.* (New York: F.W. Dodge, 1959).

Editors of Sunset Books and Sunset Magazine. *Los Angeles Portrait of an Extraordinary City.* (Menlo Park: Lane Magazine & Book Company, 1973).

Ford, James and Katherine Morrow Ford. *The Modern House In America.* (New York: Architectural Book Publishing Co., 1940).

Ford, Katherine Morrow and Thomas H. Creighton. *Quality Budget Houses.* (New York: Reinhold, 1954).

Gebhard, David and Harriette Von Breton. *Los Angeles in the Thirties: 1931-1941.* (Los Angeles, Hennessey & Ingalls, Inc., 1989).

Hess, Alan. *Googie Redux: Ultramodern Roadside Architecture.* (San Francisco: Chronicle Books, 2004).

Hess, Alan. *The Ranch House.* (New York: Harry N. Abrams, 2005).

Hess, Alan and Andrew Danish. *Palm Springs Weekend.* (San Francisco: Chronicle Books, 2001).

Hise, Greg. *Magnetic Los Angeles: Planning the Twentieth-Century Metropolis.* (Baltimore: The Johns Hopkins University Press, 1997).

Jackson, Lesley. *Contemporary.* (New York: Phaidon Press, Inc., 1994).

May, Cliff. *Western Ranch Houses by Cliff May.* (Menlo Park: Sunset Books, 1958).

Nelson, George. *Problems of Design.* (Whitney Publications Inc., 1957).

Nelson, George and Henry Wright. *Tomorrow's House.* (New York: Simon and Schuster, 1945).

Phoenix, Charles. *Cruising the Pomona Valley.* (Pomona: Horn of Plenty Press, 1999).

Roger, Kate Ellen. *The Modern House, U.S.A.* (New York: Harper & Row, 1962).

Treib, Marc and Dorothee Imbert. *Modern Landscapes for Living.* (Berkeley and Los Angeles: University of California Press, 1997).

Yorke, Francis Reginald Stevens. *The Modern House.* (Great Britain: The Architectural Press, 1934).

Periodicals

Architectural Forum, April 1943
Architectural Forum, June 1950
Architectural Forum, August 1950
Arts & Architecture, May 1948
House & Home, January 1954
House & Home, May 1957
Living for Young Homemakers, September 1957
Popular Science, December 1953

Websites

arapahoeacres.org
astroluxe.org
balboahighlands.com
crestwoodla.com
eichlernetwork.com
eichlersocal.com
laconservancy.org
marvistatract.org
preservationnation.org
ranchostyle.com
socalmodern.com

john eng

John Eng is a writer, director, designer, and photographer living a 1960s Modern life. He grew up in Queens, New York, and attended The Brooklyn Museum Art School, Parsons School of Design, and The School of Visual Arts before working in animation and special effects for television promos and commercials.

When he relocated to Los Angeles in 1981, he produced and shot several live-action, independent feature films in addition to animation work for television. In the 1990s, he directed numerous animated television shows including *Duckman* and *Jonny Quest*. After 2000, John worked in both feature and TV animation. Projects include *Rugrats Go Wild, Jimmy Neutron, The Barnyard, Hoodwinked 2, Alpha and Omega, Curious George 2,* and *Lionelville*.

John's photography has appeared in *LA Magazine, Dwell, CA Modern* magazine, *Stern* magazine, and his own website, astroluxe.org.

John has also co-authored two books with Adriene Biondo, *Southern California Eats* and *Southern California Eats 2.*

adriene biondo

A preservationist and photographer, Adriene worked with the City of Los Angeles and Los Angeles Conservancy to create a historic district for the 1963-64 Balboa Highlands Eichler tract where she and John Eng make their home. She was also a member of the Historic Quest Committee in San Francisco, which was honored with a President's Award for qualifying the Green Gables and Greenmeadow Eichler tracts for the National Register. Adriene has worked with The Getty Conservation Institute and contributed to *SurveyLA*, part of a broader collaboration with the City of Los Angeles funded by The Getty. Adriene's focus on historic preservation presents her with endless opportunities to combine her passions, from documenting the urban landscape to photography. Her work can be seen in a variety of publications, including the National Trust's "Los Angeles Modern: City of Tomorrow" booklet.

[...] revolutionary design
[...] the most talked about,
[...] mes in the world.

[...] nd home-building or-
[...] m almost every great
[...] ler the most honored

[...] from the American
[...] ts and Sunset Magazine

[...] e of Architects and Sunset Maga-
[...] er Homes as worthy of important

[...] y pleased when homes in the West
[...] ey rate the attention of a distin-
[...] om all parts of the country..."
[...] set Magazine letter to Eichler Homes

EICHLER HOMES

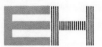

2151 ST. FRANCIS DRIVE • PALO ALTO, CALIFORNIA • DAvenport 1-1720

May 6, 1962

Folks:

This is to inform you that we have broken ground on our long-awaited project in the San Fernando Valley, to be known as Eichler Homes' Balboa Highlands. It is located in Granada Hills, on Balboa Boulevard, almost directly across, and starting about 100 feet north, of the Knollwood Country Club and Golf Course. On gently rolling land, most of the lots provide magnificent views. It is approximately 4 or 5 minutes ride to either the San Diego or Golden State Freeways, with schools, shopping centers, parks and churches close by.

Balboa Highlands buyers will have a choice of 4 beautiful floor plans, all with the famous atrium or forecourt that distinguishes an Eichler home, ranging in size from 1875 to 2531 square feet, and including refrigerated air-conditioning. In addition, all utilities will be underground, so that there will never be seen the unsightly telephone poles, and overhead wiring, that mar so many subdivisions.

We expect to have our model homes ready for the official grand opening in about 60 to 75 days. Temporary offices have been opened at 13535 Ventura Boulevard, Suite 204, in Sherman Oaks..State 9-8185. Floor plans and site maps of the first 51 lots are here for your perusal prior to the advertised opening for the general public.

Hoping to hear from you in the near future, I remain,

Sincerely yours,

Nat Granat

Nat Granat
Community Sales Manager.

Sat. opt -
2:00 p.m.

Woodman ave -
20 % -

opt 2 -
31950
. 70
6 3 90.0 0

Letter and newspaper advertisement announcing the availability of new homes in the Balboa Highlands Eichler Tract in Granada Hills and the Fairhaven Tract in Orange County. Original brochure courtesy Ann Ziliak.

Now you can live in an
EICHLER HOME!

Just

shop
a
Chu
Natura
too

SEE
Santa An
on 17th t
left on Gr
FAIRHA

FRI., FEB. 5, 1960 Los Angeles Times

GRAND OPENING!
Great News! Award-winning
EICHLER HOMES
come to Southern California!
FAIRHAVEN
in the beautiful City of Orange

Original postcard from Eichler Homes. Photo by Ernest Braun.

ELEVATIONS

TRACT 14944

CRESTWOOD HILLS

MUTUAL HOUSING ASSOCIATION INC.

WHITNEY R SMITH   A. QUINCY JONES   EDGARDO CONTINI

ASSOCIATED ARCHITECTS AND ENGINEER

EXECUTIVE OFFICE
626 NORTH ROBERTSON
LOS ANGELES 46
CRESTVIEW 5-3175   BRADSHAW 2-4159

DATE 12-10-48	APPROVED
REV. MAL 3-28-49	
MALF 5-25-49	
5-30-49	

| DRAWN D.M.W. | SHEET NUMBER |
| CHECKED | **4** |

N ↑